An Introduction to Schools of Economic Thought

Hobart Paperback 223

About the IEA

Founded in 1955, the Institute of Economic Affairs is Britain's oldest free market think tank. Its mission is to improve understanding of the fundamental institutions of a free society by analysing and expounding the role of markets in solving economic and social problems.

The IEA publishes numerous peer-reviewed books and papers each year as well as shorter briefings. Much of this work is freely available on the IEA website: **www.iea.org.uk**.

The IEA's peer-reviewed academic journal – which it produces with the University of Buckingham, Universidad Francisco Marroquín and Universidad de las Hespérides – is published by Wiley. To receive regular updates on the IEA's work, you can subscribe to our Substack at **insider.iea.org.uk**.

AN INTRODUCTION TO SCHOOLS OF ECONOMIC THOUGHT

EAMONN BUTLER

Institute of
Economic Affairs

First published in Great Britain in 2025 by
The Institute of Economic Affairs
2 Lord North Street
Westminster
London SW1P 3LB
in association with London Publishing Partnership Ltd
www.londonpublishingpartnership.co.uk

The mission of the Institute of Economic Affairs is to improve understanding of the fundamental institutions of a free society by analysing and expounding the role of markets in solving economic and social problems.

Copyright © The Institute of Economic Affairs 2025

The moral rights of the authors have been asserted.

All rights reserved. Without limiting the rights under copyright reserved above, no part of this publication may be reproduced, stored or introduced into a retrieval system, or transmitted, in any form or by any means (electronic, mechanical, photocopying, recording or otherwise), without the prior written permission of both the copyright owner and the publisher of this book.

A CIP catalogue record for this book is available from the British Library.

ISBN 978-0-255-36848-3

Many IEA publications are translated into languages other than English or are reprinted. Permission to translate or to reprint should be sought from the Executive Director at the address above.

Typeset in Kepler by T&T Productions Ltd
www.tandtproductions.com

Cover illustration: *Market Scene*, 1832, George Wilfred Anthony.
The Walters Art Museum.

Printed and bound by Hobbs the Printers Ltd

CONTENTS

	About the author	viii
	Foreword	ix
1	**Introduction**	1
	The role of this book	1
	What is a school of thought?	2
	Why study the schools of economics?	2
	What this book covers	3
2	**Preclassical economics**	6
	The first economists	6
	Commerce versus authority	7
	The mercantilist era	8
3	**The Classical School**	10
	Overview	10
	Adam Smith	11
	Thomas Malthus	21
	David Ricardo	22
	James and John Stuart Mill	26
	The French Laissez-Faire economists	27
	Relevance today	30
4	**Karl Marx**	31
	The critique of capitalism	31
	Criticism and legacy	35

5 Marginalism and the Neoclassical synthesis — 39
- The Marginal Revolution — 39
- The Neoclassical School — 42
- Key figures of the Neoclassical School — 44
- Criticism and contemporary extension — 48

6 Keynes and the Keynesians — 50
- Keynes's contribution — 50
- Background to Keynes's ideas — 51
- Keynes's analysis and prescriptions — 52
- Neo-Keynesians — 55

7 The Chicago School — 58
- Principles — 58
- Origins — 61
- Monetarism — 62
- Rational Expectations Theory — 65
- Human Capital Theory — 67
- Supply-Side Economics — 69
- Criticisms — 71
- Conclusion — 72

8 The Austrian School — 74
- Origin and principles — 74
- Subjectivism versus Keynesianism — 77
- Time, uncertainty and ignorance — 78
- Doubts on interventionism — 83
- Criticisms and responses — 85
- The fruitfulness of Austrian insights — 87

9 The Public Choice School — 89
- Origins — 90
- The peculiarity of the political 'market' — 91

Self-interest in the political system	92
Decisions and constitutions	97
The impact of the Public Choice School	99
10 Behavioural Economics	**101**
Biases in human decision-making	101
Implications of thought biases	107
General criticism and legacy	110
11 The future and the past	**112**
Future schools of thought?	112
Conclusion: strength through diversity	113
References	**115**
Further reading	116
About the IEA	**120**

ABOUT THE AUTHOR

Eamonn Butler is Director of the Adam Smith Institute, one of the world's leading policy think tanks. He holds degrees in economics and psychology, a PhD in philosophy and an honorary DLitt. In the 1970s he worked in Washington, DC, for the US House of Representatives, and taught philosophy at Hillsdale College, Michigan, before returning to the UK to co-found the Adam Smith Institute. He has won the Freedom Medal of Freedoms Foundation at Valley Forge, the UK National Free Enterprise Award and the Hayek Institute Lifetime Achievement Award; his film *Secrets of the Magna Carta* won an award at the Anthem Film Festival; and his book *Foundations of a Free Society* won the Fisher Prize.

Eamonn's other books include introductions to the pioneering economists Adam Smith, Milton Friedman, F. A. Hayek and Ludwig von Mises, and primers on a wide range of topics, including capitalism, classical liberalism, democracy, economic inequality, public choice, taxation, trade, the Austrian School of Economics and great liberal thinkers. He has also published *The Condensed Wealth of Nations* and *The Best Book on the Market*, and is co-author of *Forty Centuries of Wage and Price Controls* and a series of books on IQ. He is a frequent contributor to print, broadcast and online media.

FOREWORD

Studying economics – especially at university – can be a sterile and lifeless endeavour. In four out of five classes, you will essentially just go from one mathematical model, which attempts to represent some aspect of economic life, to the next mathematical model, which attempts to represent a different aspect of economic life. The mathematical, model-based approach is by no means without merits. The problem is that it comes with high opportunity costs: it crowds out many other things.

One of its casualties is the fact that economics, as a discipline, has forgotten its own history. I studied economics for six years but learned virtually nothing about *why* we were doing things the way we did. Where did this approach come from? Had economics always been this way? Are there now, or were there ever, any alternative approaches? The names of prominent economic thinkers sometimes made cameo appearances, but only when a formula or a graph was named after them.

That is why Mark Skousen's book *The Making of Modern Economics*, which is about the lives and contributions of the great economists from Adam Smith to Milton Friedman, was such a revelation to me at the time. (It was first published in 2001; I must have discovered it four or five years later.) It managed to bring economics to life, presenting it as a battle of ideas rather than a succession of formulas.

Eamonn Butler's book *An Introduction to Schools of Economic Thought* can fulfil a similar role today. Butler's approach is somewhat different from Skousen's: rather than focusing on individual economists, Butler groups them together into major *schools* of economic thought.

A school of thought, in this context, is not simply a bunch of people who share common research interests, or who favour similar economic policies (although they may do that as well). They often differ on a more fundamental level. They differ on questions such as the following:

- What is economics?
- Is economics more like a natural science, such as physics or chemistry? Or is it more like a social science, such as political science or history?
- Should economics aim to be value-neutral? Or should economists concern themselves with questions of ethics and morality?
- What is the appropriate unit of economic analysis? Is that the individual, presumed to be an autonomous agent? Or is it a collective, such as a social class or power structure?
- To what extent should economics be a self-contained discipline, and to what extent should it borrow from others, such as psychology? Should economists narrowly focus on their bread-and-butter topics, such as GDP growth, employment, inflation and productivity? Or can economic logic be usefully

applied to social phenomena, such as crime and family structure, which we do not usually think of as 'economics'?
- If I want to be an expert in the British economy of the 2020s, do I need to know much about British culture, politics, history and institutions? Or can an outside observer attain the same level of expertise, just by studying the relevant economic data?

In short, to say that X and Y subscribe to different schools of economic thought does not just mean that they disagree on whether the additional rate of income tax should be abolished, or on whether Britain should rejoin the European Economic Area. (Members of different schools of thought may well agree on those issues – if for different reasons.) What it means is that they differ on a more general level, in how they think about economics.

Some schools of thought are complementary: a member of the Public Choice School or Virginia School, for example, can also be a member of the Chicago School. Others are mutually exclusive: a member of the Austrian School, for example, cannot also be a Marxist. In other cases, it is possible to straddle a divide, but it would involve some tension. Some are rivals, some are allies, some are friendly rivals, some are orthogonal to each other.

Eamonn Butler is, of course, not a detached, impartial observer in all this. But while the reader will probably be able to guess where Butler's sympathies lie, he nonetheless represents each school of thought accurately and fairly. His aim is to provide a meta-level overview of these schools, not to recruit the reader into any one of them.

The IEA is not a detached, impartial observer either. The list of IEA authors over the years contains many of the leading lights of the Austrian School (Friedrich Hayek, Israel Kirzner), the Chicago School (Milton Friedman, George Stigler, Ronald Coase, Gary Becker) and the Public Choice School (James Buchanan, Gordon Tullock). Nonetheless, while individual IEA staff members or authors may well identify with one particular school of economic thought or other, the IEA as such has never been 'an Austrian Economics think tank', 'a Chicago School think tank' or 'a Public Choice School think tank'. It is a broad church in the parish of Classical Liberalism, which people can reach via Chicago, Vienna, Virginia, or indeed from plenty of other directions.

KRISTIAN NIEMIETZ
Editorial Director, Institute of Economic Affairs
May 2025

1 INTRODUCTION

The role of this book

This book explains some of the most significant approaches to the problems of economics, from early history to the present day. It shows how and why different thinkers have come up with different explanations of how economic life operates and how we might improve its workings to boost human prosperity and welfare.

The book is written in accessible language. It is aimed at lay readers who want to understand how economics developed, and the debates that still rage between different economists.

It should also be helpful to school and university students who want to explore different ideas and gain a broader view of economics than they find in their textbooks, which usually say little about other approaches to economics and how they arose or were abandoned. But each different approach to economic thought has something to teach us about how people make choices, which is what economics is, or should be, about.

What is a school of thought?

In economics, a *school of thought* is a group of economists who share a broadly common perspective on how to study economic phenomena, and which features of economic life are most important. But within that, they may focus on different subtopics, use different methods and reach different conclusions.

Members of different schools of economics may self-identify as such, or they might be placed within those schools by others. Schools are not formal associations like a club or society, but emerge organically when thinkers cluster around shared ideas, methods or questions – often led there by influential books, articles or thinkers.

Why study the schools of economics?

By focusing on schools of thought, we can understand the broader intellectual currents in economics, the debates they spark, and their impact on the real world. This provides useful context against which we can evaluate and critique current economic theories and policy proposals. It helps us understand past economic trends, structures and problems, and why so many past explanations have proved inadequate. It helps us learn useful lessons about the nature of economic events such as depressions, booms and bubbles, giving us insights into what policies might help create stability and growth – and to avoid future mistakes.

The different schools of economic thought developed within the conditions of the time: the laws, politics, culture, customs, institutions, conflicts and other features of human life. Understanding how economists navigated these different realities helps us analyse the role of such factors in shaping our economic life. That in turn helps us understand our own times and improve our policies and institutions. And by placing economics within the wider context of human life, it helps us appreciate the benefits of economics working alongside political science, psychology, and other social sciences, and so gain a deeper understanding of human action.

What this book covers

Ancient and medieval economics. This book starts (chapter 2) with the insight that economic activity, as represented by international trade, can be traced back at least 20,000 years and is undoubtedly far older. But this was all taken for granted: few people asked how or why it happened, or thought about it systematically, until the Ancient Greeks, and not many others for centuries after that.

Classical School. Chapter 3 explores the more scientific approach of the eighteenth and nineteenth centuries, with *Classical School* thinkers such as Adam Smith and David Ricardo. They identified many principles that economists use today, such as the roles of specialisation, exchange, prices and capital. They established economics as an independent discipline – perhaps even a science. Yet they struggled with the traditional idea that what gave goods their *value* was the amount of *labour* used to produce them. They remained unsatisfied with this *labour theory of value*, unlike *Karl Marx* (chapter 4), who would later found an entire economic philosophy on it.

Marginalism and the Neoclassical synthesis. Long before then, though, economic thinking had moved on. Economics was revolutionised by the realisation that value was not a fixed *objective* property of goods, such as weight or colour, but the *subjective* opinion of the valuer. Value is in the eye of the beholder: which is why a sketch that took Picasso only moments to produce can sell for hundreds of thousands of dollars.

Another insight was *marginalism* – that consumers did not value each unit of a good *equally* but tended to value *additional* units *less*. (There are only so many cabbages or chocolates one can consume and still enjoy the next one.)

The *Neoclassical School* (chapter 5) would synthesise this *subjectivist* and *marginalist* thinking with the broad principles of the Classical School, using mathematics to reach sophisticated conclusions about economic phenomena. This approach would dominate the field through most of the twentieth century.

Keynes versus Chicago. Neoclassical economists thought that markets, and the economy in general, would tend automatically towards balance (or *equilibrium*). This proved over-optimistic, as demonstrated by various economic crises, including the Great Depression of the 1930s. Consequently, there developed (chapter 6) a much more interventionist view, in which John Maynard Keynes and his followers argued that governments needed to work actively to maintain economic stability. This in turn was challenged by members of the *Chicago School* (chapter 7), notably the arch-*monetarist* Milton Friedman.

The reality of decision-making. In contrast to the Keynesians and the Chicago and Neoclassical economists, the *Austrian School* (chapter 8) used subjectivist and marginalist insights to create a wholly different approach to how people made choices, how those choices should be studied, and the limits to our understanding of them.

The *Public Choice School*, which arose in the mid twentieth century (chapter 9), was also sceptical. They used the tools of economics to demonstrate the institutional flaws in how governments implement economic policies. Now it was the more interventionist Keynesians who looked over-optimistic.

The book continues (chapter 10) by reviewing a recent development, *Behavioural Economics*, which brings human psychology squarely into economic choices. And it concludes with a speculation (chapter 11) about the future direction of economics and the new schools of thought that might emerge.

2 PRECLASSICAL ECONOMICS

The ancient world was surprisingly active economically. There is evidence of active trade around Indonesia 20,000 years ago. Copper mined in England 3,500 years ago was being sold throughout Europe, while northern European amber was exported as far as Egypt. Islanders from South-East Asia were taking goods, crops and spices to and from India. Chinese tea was spreading across the world.

Yet nobody sought to explain *how* or *why* all this happened. It was simply taken for granted. The Old Testament, for example, describes specialisation, trade, exchange and money; but it has no *economic theory* of these things, focusing only on the ethical issues. Ancient Egypt abounded with written commercial records and price lists, but again there were no written *explanations* of how prices came about.

The first economists

The first significant economic theorising arose in Ancient Greece. Ethics remained the principal concern, but Plato (*c.* 427–348 BC) wrote about wealth, money, inequality, lending at interest, business regulation and specialisation.

His student Aristotle (384–22 BC) would become the first systematic *economist*, coining the word *Oikonomica* ('economics'), from *oikos* ('household') and *nomos* ('rule' or 'management'). Among other insights, Aristotle talked of the merits of specialisation; contrasted *money* with *capital goods* that boost future production; sought to justify the institution of private property; and saw money as not just a store of value but a facilitator of exchange.

Aristotle worried, though, that the use of money in economic exchange raised ethical problems. Every object, he explained, has two uses. A shoe is for wearing, but it can also be exchanged for money: but exchange for money (he thought) would enrich the seller at the expense of the buyer. (It would be over a thousand years before others explained why this was wrong.) And to Aristotle, the worst form of exchange was money lending. Economics, he thought, should be about serving our needs, not accumulating wealth. (This 'usury' issue would trouble economists for the next *two* thousand years.)

Commerce versus authority

Like Aristotle, the Early Christian *Scholastics* such as St Augustine (345–430) focused on ethics and warned against commercial greed. But commerce was spreading, and eventually St Thomas Aquinas (*c.* 1225–74) sought to make Church law reflect economic reality. He accepted that possession was natural, and that private property was better looked after than public assets: but he insisted that property must be used ethically, in accordance with divine law.

Like all before them, the Scholastics struggled to understand *prices*. They imagined that every good possessed a certain value, so only goods of *equal* value could be exchanged justly. But how to determine the 'just price' (i.e. exchange value) of the multitude of traded goods? We can only estimate it, Aquinas conceded: and anyway, it would vary due to unseen factors like transport costs. And on usury, likewise, he thought that a premium could be charged to reflect the risk of not being repaid, or because higher returns could be gained elsewhere (*opportunity cost* as modern economists call it), thus reconciling *lending at interest* with Canon Law.

But the Church's authority over economic life was fading. Revolutions in capital finance, maritime discoveries, and the sheer growth of trade and commerce outpaced the clergy's objections. Henceforth, economics would be a *secular* science.

The mercantilist era

Late medieval rulers raised revenues through taxes and by selling monopolies in both domestic production and foreign trade. They established colonies to secure the supply of gold and silver and other important items. And they thought, on the lines of Aristotle, that a country would become rich only by taking gold and silver from others, through trade (or, sometimes, conquest).

This thinking produced *mercantilism*, an approach to trade that dominated Europe through the seventeenth and eighteenth centuries. Its ultimate objective was to maximise national strength, and the wealth earned from selling goods abroad was seen as the basis of that strength. So countries obsessed on promoting their exports to earn gold and silver, while minimising their imports, which would cost them this 'treasure'. National strength was seen as so important that no trade restriction was off limits. Imports were taxed or banned, while export industries were subsidised. Even individual towns adopted the same policy, restricting commerce to reduce their dependence on other communities.

But mercantilism had its critics. The French Physiocrat economists, led by François Quesnay (1694–1774) and Anne-Robert-Jacques Turgot (1727–81), argued that wealth was in fact created by *productive work* – specifically in agriculture. As Controller-General of Finances to King Louis XVI, Turgot sought to encourage such enterprise by removing many regulations and price controls. He even suspended controls on usury, cleverly explaining that high interest rates may reflect the scarcity of savings, the time needed to establish production and the uncertainty of the result: lenders were therefore not just idle funders but skilled entrepreneurs, balancing risk and profit.

This, then, was the state of economics up to that time: more a practical pursuit than a scientific one. But there would soon be an intellectual revolution.

3 THE CLASSICAL SCHOOL

Overview

The eighteenth century, and the decades either side of it, were an age of enlightenment. Theorists began to think systematically about the workings of human life and society. They focused on how economies operate and grow, creating the framework within which later economics would develop. The main exponents of what became known as the *Classical School* of economics were Adam Smith (1723–90), David Ricardo (1772–1823), Thomas Malthus (1766–1834) and James Mill (1773–1836).

The Classical School focused on long-term economic realities. They believed that free individuals, pursuing their own interests, would generate prosperity both for themselves and indeed for everyone. They argued that regulation of trade and commerce often stifled economic progress; and they thought that if markets failed to achieve such progress, the most likely explanation was inept interventions by politicians. They saw government as more properly a referee rather than an economic player, insisting that its power should be limited to providing defence and justice, and to setting the conditions – such as property rights, the rules of contract and infrastructure provision – that enabled the 'system of natural liberty' to deliver its economic benefits.

Adam Smith

Adam Smith arguably deserves a chapter to himself, so profound was his influence on all future economists. He is to economics what Newton is to physics or Darwin is to biology, a pioneer who created a wholly new way of looking at things. Thanks to the impressive learning he acquired over a lifetime – he has been called *the last person to know everything* – he was able to marshal a vast array of facts and theories into a radically new, comprehensive analysis of the whole range of economic phenomena and their interrelationships. Among other things that modern economists still study, he explored value, specialisation, exchange, prices, supply, demand, production, distribution, and more. He was not the first economist, but in weaving his own and others' insights together, he achieved a larger and deeper understanding of economic life. Therefore, he certainly justifies his designation as 'the father of economics' as we know the subject today.

In his great book, *An Inquiry into the Nature and Causes of the Wealth of Nations* (1776), Smith focused on how prosperity was created. The answer, as he argued with force, eloquence and a dry humour, was not the *mercantilist* way, with its controls on free exchange, designed to amass gold and silver at the expense of other nations. It was, on the contrary, to *lift restrictions* and unleash the wealth-creating capacities of free citizens. He recognised, what others had overlooked, that *free exchange benefits both sides*. For sure, the *sellers* end up financially richer: but exchange makes the *buyers* better off too, in that they gain access to the goods and services that they value. Indeed, neither side would voluntarily agree to any bargain, unless they each felt themselves a gainer. Free, uninterrupted trade and commerce, therefore, would create value for everyone involved in it, and thereby spread prosperity throughout the community and the world.

And how to measure this prosperity? Smith's answer is found on the very first page of his *Wealth of Nations*. The wealth of a nation, he says, is measured by what its people produce. He notes that larger populations will of course produce proportionately more; and that some people (e.g. the very old and the very young) may not produce anything at all. Thus, in his first few paragraphs, with breathtaking originality, Smith had invented the measures that modern economists rely on and that we now know as *Gross Domestic Product* (GDP), *GDP per capita* and *productivity*.

Productivity from specialisation

But these are just the first of many astonishing insights that Smith advances in his remarkable book. He also recognised what most of his predecessors had overlooked, that a key driver of this prosperity was the huge productivity gains made possible by *specialisation* – or as he called it, the *division of labour*.

Pin making, to take his example, may seem a 'trifling' process, but it is actually very sophisticated. Wire must be drawn out, straightened, cut and pointed. The top must be ground flat for the head, which in turn must be made and affixed. The pins must be whitened and packed. There are about eighteen different operations in the process. A single person, doing all these different tasks, might struggle to make even 20 pins a day. But by dividing the work between skilled specialists – with the right tools – a pin factory can make 50,000 pins in a day. That is because people doing the same task many times become highly skilled; it becomes worthwhile for them to own specialist equipment that can raise their output even more; and they waste less time moving from one activity to another.

Specialisation is so productive, Smith continues, that it arises not just within industries, but between them. Farmers become skilled specialists in raising crops, rather than in making household items; but manufacturers are happy to supply farmers with household goods and leave food production to them. Countries, too, export the goods they can produce more efficiently, and buy goods that others produce better or more cheaply. And, contrary to mercantilist thinking, this creates value all round. For example, Smith says, with glasshouses and other aids, it is possible to grow grapes in cold and rainy Scotland. But it is *much* cheaper for Scots to buy their grapes and grape products from balmy France. Why make yourself what you can buy more cheaply from others? Such mercantilist thinking was hardly (in his word) 'prudent'.

As with the pin makers, specialisation allows us to create large surpluses of the things we produce, which we can then use to exchange with others, benefiting both sides. And more widely, in Smith's view, this specialisation and exchange binds us all into a worldwide, cooperative network. Even a simple woollen coat, he explained, involved a 'great multitude' of specialists. Shepherds, wool-sorters, dyers, weavers, shippers, toolmakers and countless others 'all must join in their different arts in order to complete even this homely production.' Such peaceful, commercial collaboration of highly efficient specialists was the true source of prosperity.

The role of exchange

Smith accepts that, through exchange, we seek to promote only our own self-interest. But we achieve that only by serving the self-interest of others. 'It is not from the benevolence of the butcher, the brewer, or the baker, that we expect our dinner,' he wrote, 'but from their regard to their own interest.'

This was another remarkable insight: that economic self-interest, specialisation and exchange are the foundations of worldwide peaceful collaboration and prosperity. Nobody, in their bargaining, intends to promote this beneficial social end; yet it happens. As Smith noted, the 'higgling and bargaining of the market' establishes market *prices*; and where prices are high, people's pursuit of gain draws their effort and resources into their most valued uses, and away from less valued ones. This simple, automatic system creates social benefit out of individual self-interest, maximising the value generated for all involved, as if – in his memorable phrase – the process was led by an 'invisible hand' to achieve that happy result.

Just how far specialisation can go depends on the extent of the market, Smith reasoned. Great towns spring up because only they have enough customers to support specialist professions (such as porters), while scattered communities may be unable to support even basic specialists such as carpenters or builders. And in particular, cities can support banks, which further reinforce specialisation by providing people of all classes with the funds to establish new wealth-generating businesses. The use of money, he notes, is another key factor in the expansion of specialisation and market exchange. Economic life would be far less efficient in a barter economy where hungry brewers always had to search out thirsty bakers. The more widely we can exchange our surplus product for money, and then exchange that money back for the other products that we want, the faster our prosperity accelerates.

The limits of intervention

Because specialisation and free exchange create such enormous economic and social benefits, Smith argued, to restrict them through mercantilist controls, taxes, official privileges and regulations is a mistake, since it reduces their effectiveness at generating prosperity. He examined systematically all the trade policies in the mercantilist toolbox and found them, not just wanting, but harmful. So too were restrictions on domestic commerce, such as the granting of monopolies or the long apprenticeships imposed by merchants' guilds in order to restrict the availability of specialist tradespeople and so keep prices high.

By contrast, Smith's prescription for prosperity was *market freedom*, which required the existence of *private property* and its *free exchange*, with *enforceable contracts*, and market-enhancing *institutions* such as an impartial system of justice. It also required *less intervention* from governments. A great deal of harmful regulation, he thought, arose from the cronyism between politicians and business leaders who were keen to keep out the competition; and it was poorer people who would suffer most from this corruption.

Smith was an early critic of the mercantilist notion that Britain's empire was essential to its prosperity, and he called his country's attempt to prevent the American colonists trading with anyone else a 'crime against humanity'. It was only months after *The Wealth of Nations* was published that the colonists revolted against these and other 'abuses and usurpations', and Smith regretted that his arguments had not come quickly enough to head off the crisis. But the influence of his book would continue to grow, sparking the lower-tax, lower-regulation policies that would produce the great nineteenth-century era of free trade.

Certainly, Smith thought, some government activity was needed: to provide defence and a justice system, and to promote the creation of the infrastructure that commerce needed but which was difficult to finance privately. And all this would require some level of taxation. But much of the taxation of his time was levied for the benefit of the authorities rather than with any thought to its justice or effectiveness. So, he offered a practical (and enduring) set of principles for taxation. The first was *fairness* – tax should be levied according to people's ability to pay, so that it did not fall most heavily on the poorest. It should also have *certainty* – the tax that an individual owes should be clear, and not arbitrary or capricious. *Convenience* was a third principle – taxes should be collected at a time and in a way that is 'most likely to be convenient for the contributor to pay it.' And the last was *economy* – or efficiency as we might say today: a tax should not require large bureaucracies to collect it, nor discourage productive work, but should be designed to raise its revenue with the minimum of cost and economic distortion. These principles are still cited in debates on taxation today.

The Classical theory of value

Like all that had gone before them, the Classical economists struggled to identify the source and measure of value. To Smith, as with earlier writers, the obvious measure of an item's value was the *labour* put into its production. Indeed, he wrote that labour was the original source of 'all the necessaries and conveniences of life'.

Yet the puzzle remained, that something essentially useless (like diamonds) had a high *value in exchange* but little *value in use*; while something essential (like water) with a high *value in use*, had little or no *value in exchange*.

Unknown to Smith, other economists were already working on radically different solutions, though it would be another century before those solutions were generally accepted. Meanwhile, Smith saw little option but to accept the *labour theory of value* – put simply, that the value of a thing reflected the effort invested to create it. Thus, if among hunters, 'it usually costs twice the labour to kill a beaver which it does to kill a deer,' he wrote, then 'one beaver should naturally exchange for or be worth two deer.' But it was obvious that things did *not* in fact exchange in proportion to the labour invested in them. Something else must be at work. So what explained the difference?

The deer–beaver sort of trade-off, Smith suggested, applied only in the 'rude state' where labour was the *sole factor of production*. Things changed when *capital* and *land* ownership became involved. The owners of land and capital (e.g. tools, equipment and machinery) would hope to capture some of the value created by the workers' labour, because their land was necessary for production and their capital made the labour more productive. In other words, Smith was already amending the labour theory into a rough *cost of production* theory, where value reflects a mixture of labour, profit and rent.

This idea, though still a poor explanation of value, was of much wider importance to our understanding of economic life. For one thing, it suggested that *all* sections of society – not just the elite landowners and capital owners, but ordinary *workers* too – contributed to the nation's production and prosperity. This was a radical non-elitist view of society, and another reason to prune back the political power, corruption and cronyism that made workers' labour less productive and trapped them in poverty.

Value in exchange

But since Smith put *specialisation* and *exchange* at the heart of the wealth-creating process, his real focus was *value in exchange*. Money, he thought, was a poor measure of that, as the values of the precious metals used for money themselves fluctuate. Labour, even with all the qualifications he thought necessary on it, still seemed the only plausible measure.

Yet Smith was well aware of the inconsistencies between a product's cost of production (which he called the *natural* price) and the price it commands in exchange (the *market price*). Market prices, he argued, would be influenced by other factors, such as higher or lower levels of people's demand for a product. But while market prices fluctuate, he thought they would nevertheless tend to settle back to the *natural* price.

Despite Smith's best efforts, he knew that the labour theory still struggled to fit the facts of economic reality. But those efforts made him go on to think more deeply about how wealth was *distributed* between the factors of production. Wages, he thought, would reflect what workers needed to subsist, though supply and demand would also affect them. Profits too depended on the state of supply and demand, plus on other factors such as difficulty and risk. All these ideas have shaped how we think about the determination of wages, profits and prices today.

Conclusion

Smith made many other observations in *The Wealth of Nations*. But they all rest upon what we would now call *capitalism* (the word was unknown in 1776), and the remarkable productivity of specialisation and exchange. What he described, for the first time, was a fully integrated economic *network* to which all classes (workers, capital owners and land holders) contributed, the interests of each being dependent on the others.

Smith was perhaps the first person to articulate a theory of economic growth led by the *accumulation of capital*: the tools, machinery, infrastructure and other goods that make our labour more productive. He realised that *saving* was necessary for such accumulation. With his invisible hand metaphor, he explained how self-interested personal objectives, and our efforts to steer them through the objectives of others, spontaneously produced an overall social order – a market economy – that benefited everyone. He showed how 'the system of natural liberty' would enable the individuals in a market economy to maximise value for everyone engaged in it, while government interventions and regulations (often promoted by established businesses for their own benefit) would stifle value creation and reduce prosperity, particularly for the working poor. Where taxation was necessary, he showed how to make it fair, predictable, convenient and less damaging. And through all this, he saw economic life as a *moral* activity that makes markets not just efficient, but *human*.

Thomas Malthus

The English economist and cleric Thomas Malthus shared much of Smith's intellectual framework, his systematic approach, his focus on long-term principles, and his belief in the morality and value-creating power of free markets. But he saw the limits on natural resources as a challenge to market-led prosperity.

Malthus argued in his 1798 book, *An Essay on the Principle of Population*, that population grows 'geometrically' (or, as we would say, *exponentially*), i.e. growing faster and faster. But food production, he thought, grows only 'arithmetically' (i.e. *linearly*). Without natural checks such as famine or disease, or human actions such as warfare or the conscious postponement of childbearing, human numbers would outstrip resources, with living standards reduced to miserable, subsistence levels.

Malthus thought that any rise in wages above subsistence levels, by raising living standards, would lead to people having more children, more of whom would survive. But this rise in population would make labour more plentiful, and wages would be pushed back down to subsistence levels once again, with the cycle repeating endlessly.

This analysis overlooked important factors that we can see today, such as the technological leaps in agriculture and transport that would make food production and distribution very much more efficient. But it had important political consequences – including harsh new legislation that regarded poverty relief as an encouragement to population growth and which instead attempted to force destitute people into work. It had intellectual consequences too: Charles Darwin credited Malthus for inspiring the 'Which ones survive?' question that led to his theory of natural selection. And another Classical economist, David Ricardo, would build on Malthus's pessimistic view of wages, giving succour to socialist thinkers such as Karl Marx (1818–83).

David Ricardo

Ricardo was not an academic like Smith, but his career in the stock exchange gave him insight into the practical workings of the real economy: it was said that he made £1 million (about £100 million today) using inside information (and seeding rumours) to speculate on the result of the Battle of Waterloo.

Though best remembered for his explanation of *comparative advantage* as the driver of international trade, Ricardo's main contribution is perhaps his investigation of how value is created and distributed between land, labour and capital, and the social classes associated with each. In contrast to Smith's historical style, Ricardo sought to make economics an abstract, mechanical science, analysing how economic phenomena arise and how they relate to each other. His efforts to work out the full implications of the Classical approach would take them to their (often bitter) conclusions.

The question of 'surplus value'

Smith had faced the problem that the profits of capital owners meant that they must extract value from workers above what they pay them in wages, though he did not suggest that they *exploited* workers, as Marx would do later.

Like Smith, Ricardo noted the contribution of capital and land to production and went on to develop a general theory of value that would explain the differences between *use value* and *exchange value*. Exchange value, he suggested, could certainly derive from *labour*, but it also reflected *scarcity*, i.e. gaps between demand and supply. That was why the exchange value of some things (e.g. rare artworks) was much greater than the labour put into them. But those, he thought, were exceptions: most economic products (e.g. clothing, furniture or tools) could be multiplied indefinitely. And in these, he concluded, the labour expended on their production was by far the main determinant of value.

Wages and profits

Ricardo softened Malthus's idea that wages would always be bid down to subsistence levels. Convention was important too, he thought; in some places, wages were higher because of habit and custom. And there were temporary deviations from labour's 'natural' price as changing events created mismatches in the supply of and demand for workers. But government, he recommended, should not interfere, yet should let the adjustment back to the natural price run its course.

On profits, Ricardo thought that uniform profit rates would emerge across industries. Any more, and new investors would come in, adding to labour demand and bidding up wages, and creating extra competition that would squeeze profits. Any less, and the opposite would occur. So profits and wages were inversely related. To him, this was not a harmonious relationship between workers and capital owners, but an antagonistic one.

Land and rent

Ricardo developed an ingenious theory of *differential rent* to explain what proportion of production was distributed to landlords. The amounts paid in rent on different parcels of land would, he said, reflect differences in their soil, situation, and other productive strengths. Landlords could extract higher rents for the most productive land, but only lower rents for the least productive – an early example of the economic principle we now call *diminishing returns*.

Better farming techniques might make poorer land more productive, but landowners would still profit; they were not noble originators of value, as the Physiocrats believed, but exploiters of their monopoly on Nature's bounty. Their interests would always oppose those of farmers, manufacturers and consumers. It was another departure from Smith's social harmony.

Comparative advantage

In an exchange economy, explained Ricardo, we generate wealth most effectively by doing what we are *relatively* better at, compared to others.

Portugal and England, to take Ricardo's example, can both produce wine, and can both produce cloth. But Portugal's much warmer climate means it can produce wine very much more cheaply than England. So it makes sense for people in Portugal to focus their labour and capital on producing wine, export it to England, and use their earnings to buy cloth from England. Even if Portugal could produce cloth cheaper than England, they would still be better to concentrate on wine making, since their relative (*comparative*) advantage in that industry is so much greater. They only have to be *relatively* better, not the *absolute* best, for this to work.

It was another good Classical argument for free trade. Rather than trying to protect domestic producers from cheaper imports, governments should allow countries to exploit their *comparative advantages*, unleashing more highly productive trade that would deliver consumers the best and cheapest products from around the world.

Summary on Ricardo

Ricardo gave Classical theory a more real-world edge, showing how prices might fluctuate because of temporary gluts and shortages. He saw how automation might displace workers and affect wages. He explored the detail of how wealth was distributed between the factors of production and the social classes associated with them.

Though he tried to salvage the labour theory of value, his realism left it even weaker. His view that economic life was driven by the *relative*, not absolute, values of things prompted future economists to focus, more productively, on *non*-labour theories of value. But the labour theory, and Ricardo's doubts about markets and focus on wages and distribution, would continue to inspire socialist thinkers.

James and John Stuart Mill

James Mill (1773–1836) was a key figure in Classical thought and its dissemination in the nineteenth century. He helped David Ricardo to publish *On the Principles of Political Economy and Taxation*, refined Ricardo's theories on value and on comparative advantage, and shared Ricardo's focus on rent, wages and profits.

Mill's book *Elements of Political Economy* (1821) wove Smith's foundational work on capital accumulation and specialisation with Ricardo's refinements on value, wages, rent and distribution, and made the resulting synthesis more intelligible to the general public. Like other Classical economists, he took a generally optimistic and non-interventionist approach.

His famous son, John Stuart Mill (1806–73), is often seen as a transitional figure between the Classical School and the Neoclassical scholars that would succeed them, focusing more on social welfare.

The French Laissez-Faire economists

Like Adam Smith, the French Laissez-Faire economists Jean-Baptiste Say (1767–1832), Frédéric Bastiat (1801–50) and later thinkers involved with the *Journal des Économistes* perhaps also deserve their own chapter. They are not regarded as part of the Classical School, though much of their thinking overlapped with it.

They were Classical Liberals who sought to rebuild the economy of post-revolution France on scientific principles. They popularised Adam Smith's ideas in France, applied them to the modern industrial world and built new insights upon them. They also shared (and sometimes exceeded) Smith's optimism about the power of markets, and his emphasis on individual liberty and limited government. Faithful to Smith's rejection of mercantilism and controls, they were influential in the liberalisation of trade in Europe, informing the 1860 Cobden–Chevalier Treaty that reduced tariffs between France and Britain.

Jean-Baptiste Say

Jean-Baptiste Say emphasised the self-correcting power of markets and the role of entrepreneurship in production. His 'law of markets' (which became known as *Say's Law* and is often summarised as 'supply creates its own demand') maintained that the production of goods creates wages, profits and rents that are then sufficient to purchase those goods. By producing things, in other words, people and firms create the purchasing power needed to buy other products.

Importantly, Say emphasised the role of *entrepreneurs* as key drivers of economic activity. He saw them as people who *organise production* by combining labour, capital and land, and as evaluating and managing risk to bring goods to market. They were, therefore, an important but overlooked factor in production and wealth creation.

Tackling the labour theory of value, Say argued, against traditional thinking, that the value of goods derives from their *utility* – i.e. how useful they are to those who consume them – rather than the labour that has gone into their production. This was a critical step towards our modern, *subjective* ideas of value, namely that value is in the eye of the beholder, not in the object itself. And it would inspire later economists, such as those of the Austrian School, who would further refine the concept.

Say was a strong proponent of laissez-faire – the idea that economic agents should be left alone, and that government intervention distorts the natural balance of markets. Free trade and competition, he thought, would optimise both resource use and prosperity.

Frédéric Bastiat

Bastiat was a leading member of the French Liberal School, which was influenced by Classical ideas. He was a staunch advocate of free markets, property rights and laissez-faire, though his writings were intended to popularise those principles, and critique protectionism, rather than to advance economic theory. But in that, he proved to be a brilliant communicator and polemicist.

His 'broken window fallacy', for example, which appeared in *That Which Is Seen, and That Which Is Not Seen* (1850), debunked the idea that destruction (e.g. in warfare) was good for boosting economic activity. If a shopkeeper's window is smashed and he pays to fix it, Bastiat argued, the glazier benefits. But that is only the 'seen' effect. The 'unseen' is what the shopkeeper *could have spent* on other things, like new shoes, had the window not been broken. (Today we would call this the *opportunity* cost.) Destruction, he concluded, does not create economic activity; it merely diverts it. This was an argument that, a century later, would be used against Keynes's idea that (even wasteful) government spending could re-boot economic growth.

Bastiat was also a very effective advocate of free trade. In *Economic Sophisms* (1846 and 1848), he used satire and logic to mock protectionism, most famously in his satirical *Candlemakers' Petition*, where candlemakers demand tariffs on sunlight to 'protect' their industry. Such protectionism, he explained, enriches a few producers at the expense consumers and the nation's overall wealth.

In his book *The Law* (1850), Bastiat argued fiercely that government's legitimate role is to protect life, liberty and property – not to redistribute wealth or intervene in markets. He saw state overreach (e.g. subsidies, tariffs) as 'legal plunder', where the authorities take from some to give to others, distorting the natural economic harmony.

The Journal des Économistes circle

The *Journal des Économistes*, founded in 1841, was a key platform for the French Liberal School, including Bastiat and followers of Say, who represented and developed Classical ideas within France. They strongly defended laissez-faire – taking it to its logical conclusions and even proposing ideas like privatising defence and security. And just as strongly, they critiqued the socialist thinking that was growing in mid-century Europe.

Relevance today

The Classical and French Laissez-Faire Schools remain very relevant today. We live in an era of expanding state control, for which Classical thinking provides an antidote, reminding us that markets, left free, align resources better than regulators and planners. It also tells us that individual self-interest can and does work to produce an overall social benefit. Its focus on long-term truths and principles brings depth to a world of near-sighted political action. And it carries a moral weight, resonating with those who believe that the enlarged state is stifling the creative genius of free individuals in a free society.

4 KARL MARX

The critique of capitalism

Despite all the problems that the Classical economists saw in the labour theory of value, their inability to provide other explanations meant that it survived surprisingly long. Indeed, it became the starting point for socialist critics of the emerging industrial system. Its simple arithmetic convinced them that capital owners (whom they dubbed *capitalists*) were unjustly extracting 'surplus' value that rightfully belonged to workers.

Accordingly, the English thinker Thomas Hodgskin (1787–1869) argued that labour was the sole source of value and should receive all of its product, while the French philosopher Pierre-Joseph Proudhon (1809–65) went further, arguing that profit, interest and rent were all forcibly extracted from workers by capitalists and should be abolished. And other socialist thinkers would elaborate on Ricardo's concern about the distribution of value between land, capital and labour. To them, this was not merely a dry fact but a set of *unjust* social relationships.

Marx's interpretation

Starting from there, Karl Marx would develop an entire sociology of production, a systematic critique of capitalism based on radically new interpretations of philosophy and history. One such foundation was *historical materialism* – the idea that the development of human societies is driven by the nature of their production processes and the class struggles that result. Marx believed that history inevitably progresses through stages based on the prevailing production methods, the major transitions being from feudalism to capitalism and then to socialism.

The social relationships of urban factory production, he observed, were very different from those in the earlier agricultural economy. Capitalist production, based on property and labour, divided society into classes – capital owners and workers. While Ricardo had explored how the value created by production was *then* divided between classes, Marx saw class divisions *within production itself*. Thus, agricultural economies produced feudal relationships, while industrial economies produced capitalist ones.

Also important to Marx was the prevailing institutional *superstructure* – the political, legal and cultural institutions, including religion, colonialism and the media culture, that the ruling class used to entrench capitalism and maintain their dominance. This, he thought, helps explain why workers accept capitalism, even though they are *exploited* by it.

The Classical thinkers, Marx believed, were wrong to assume that capitalism, and the social relationships around it, were somehow natural and permanent. History would move on, he thought, and these unjust relationships would not survive. The contradictions and class conflicts created by this capitalist system of production would bring capitalism's demise.

Surplus value and worker exploitation

Marx's critique of capitalism, outlined in his three-volume work *Capital* (1867–94), depended heavily on the idea that workers were being robbed of value – *exploited* – by the capitalists. He used the labour theory of value to argue that, since the exchange value of products equals the labour time put into them, then the exchange value of labour time (i.e. the wages paid) must equal the value of the products it creates. But in fact, the capitalists are able to sell those products for more. They were reaping a *surplus* by covertly under-rewarding workers for their effort.

The capitalists hide this exploitation in a number of ways, said Marx. For example, wages are paid at the end of the week, so the workers contribute their labour in advance, while the capitalists pay their wages in arrears. And capitalism's *commodity fetishism* – its focus on *consumption* – makes people think that products have a greater inherent value than the labour put into them. So workers do not even realise that value is being stolen from them.

This exploitation theory depended on Marx keeping alive the labour theory of value. That was not easy, given its obvious problems. For example, it was evident that unskilled labour would probably produce less than skilled labour, and take more time. But that additional time and effort cannot add to the value of the final product, as the raw labour theory would imply. To get round this problem, Marx instead suggested that the exchange value of a product would equal only the '*socially necessary* labour time' expended on it under '*normal conditions* of production'. But there is no obvious and objective way to define and measure these concepts – which merely load the labour theory with complexities in the attempt to shoehorn it to fit the facts.

Theory of economic development

On the basis of these ideas, however, Marx predicted the future development (and demise) of capitalism. The constant pressure of competition would squeeze profits, forcing firms to pursue ever-greater productivity. They would have to expand their output, which would require more and more capital, and cut their costs, which meant exploiting workers even more. Capitalists would bid wages down to mere *subsistence* levels and seek to extract greater and greater surplus by imposing longer working hours, child labour and harsher conditions.

And given the ups and downs in economic activity, firms would need an 'industrial reserve army' of workers to ensure that they could access labour in times when more was needed. But the very existence of such reserves, argued Marx, would drive wages down even further. And the more that capitalism grew, the bigger the reserve army would have to be. This was, in his words, a 'law of increasing misery'.

But capitalism contains the seeds of its own destruction. For one thing, it *alienates* workers from the products of their labour. They do not control or own what they produce – the capital owner controls and takes it. The system dehumanises workers, regarding them as mere labour power, not as individuals. Not only is that unethical; it will drive workers to overthrow capitalism.

But this was only one of capitalism's self-contradictions. Capitalists, thought Marx, could not continue to exploit workers enough to maintain the increasing capital and productivity that they needed to survive. Capitalism would suffer fatal crises, because the ever-greater pursuit of profit would lead to the overproduction of goods – far more than workers could afford. The resulting failures would contribute further to capitalism's inevitable demise. Eventually, the class conflicts inherent in capitalism would mean that workers, with their shared experience of exploitation and alienation, would develop a collective awareness of their own class interests. This would prompt them into organised resistance and revolution, bringing about the socialist phase of historical development and a new system, based on common ownership of the means of production, where production would be organised to meet human needs rather than to produce profit.

Criticism and legacy

Few economists have been impressed by Marx's reliance on the collective identity of the working class as the basis of a new collective social order. Mancur Olson (1932–98), for example, warned of the 'free rider' problem: who would exert themselves on collective production if the rewards were the same for those who did not? (The starvation created by collective farm systems in China and the Soviet Union gave the stark answer.) And does working class identity even exist, particularly to the extent of bringing about revolution? In practice, Marxist uprisings have been led by small elites rather than the collective motivation of a proletariat.

Also, Marx's idea of surplus value and worker exploitation rests on a labour theory of value whose own internal contradictions were already evident to earlier writers. Like the geocentric model of the universe, it could survive only by loading it with increasing complexities like 'socially necessary labour time'. But by then such a model becomes too convoluted to explain anything. A different, simpler explanation is needed.

Moreover, where Marx thought that ruthless competition would leave workers in subsistence-level misery, reality suggests otherwise. Average workers in the industrial economies of today enjoy standards of living that even the capital owners of Marx's time could not dream of. To take a famous example, in 1914, the carmaker Henry Ford doubled his workers' wages to $5 a day (about $160 today) in return for productivity guarantees. So, what was a rational policy for the business, boosting efficiency and worker retention, also made workers much better off – a mutual gain for both capital owners and workers that Marx did not anticipate.

Marx's ideas, therefore, fail to produce a general theory of wages, capital, profit, rent and interest for a modern economy. His followers have had to resort to ever-more complex explanations (such as colonialism and slavery) to explain the prosperity and endurance of capitalist economies. And the systems that were built upon Marx's thinking have been poor advertisements for his analysis and proposals.

Even so, Marx retains an extraordinary grip on modern intellectuals, and his ideas resonate widely with many people today. Perhaps that is because they address issues such as inequality, exploitation, alienation, and the concentration of wealth and power in a few hands, all of which are seen as problems today. Younger people, in particular, reject what they see as capitalism's pursuit of profit rather than social good, and respond to Marx's call for systemic change. And free-market ideas, reflecting Adam Smith's invisible hand explanation of how self-interested action can produce general benefits (so that the pursuit of profit *can itself be a social good*), are counterintuitive and harder to understand.

Things were quite different in Marx's own lifetime. *Capital* was dismissed as a mix of outdated economics and pseudo-sociological jargon. Within five years, the 'Marginal Revolution' would solve the water–diamonds paradox and leave the labour theory for dead. Marx himself would die in academic obscurity. As Philip Magness and Michael Mokovi (2023) have established, Marx gained few scholarly citations during his lifetime, and most of those were critical, even scornful. Interest rose only after

1917. Despite all his shortcomings, it seems, Marx's vision of a new social order provided a convenient intellectual justification for the violence and upheavals of the Russian Revolution.

5 MARGINALISM AND THE NEOCLASSICAL SYNTHESIS

The Marginal Revolution

The shortcomings of the labour theory were evident to many economists even before Marx was born. But over the course of a century, there developed a radically different approach, which became known as the Marginal Revolution. This would provide the foundation of a completely new school of economic thought, the Austrian School; and it also informed the thinking of what became the Neoclassical School, who synthesised it with the methods of the Classical economists.

The Marginal Revolution was based on two novel insights. The first was *subjectivism.* This is the idea that value was not an objective quality of an item, like its size or weight. Nor was it the labour that had gone into its production. Rather, value is an individual's personal (*subjective*) reaction to something, based on how useful they think it is to them. So, different people may value the *same* item *differently.* For example, an omnivorous diner may value an omelette as a tasty meal, while a vegan diner would not value it at all.

The second insight was *marginalism*. This is the observation that people's valuation of things is not constant. A hungry diner, for instance, might get great satisfaction from one omelette, but perhaps less from a second and probably much less from a third or fourth. The diner's satisfaction *diminishes* as additional (*marginal*) units of something are consumed. Marginalists called this *diminishing marginal utility*.

These insights turned attention away from the Classical focus on the *cost of producing* things and onto the analysis of *how people value* things – especially, how they value each *additional unit* of something. The principle of *diminishing marginal utility* became a key explanation of how people make choices, and therefore of their economic actions.

The Marginalists went on to deduce that rational individuals would continue to consume a product only until the additional satisfaction it delivered (its *marginal* utility) fell to the point where it became equal to the *marginal cost* of acquiring the product. For example, rational diners would continue to consume omelettes until they felt that the enjoyment from any more of them was not worth the cost on their budget (or perhaps their digestion).

These ideas proved very fertile, leading to the formulation of many concepts that are now fundamental principles of economic enquiry, such as *supply and demand curves*, *price theory* and *equilibrium analysis* (the investigation of how markets reach a balance between supply and demand). And their logic applies not only to the markets for *consumer goods* (like omelettes) but the markets for all the *capital goods* used to create them (such as farm equipment and frying pans).

The origins of marginalism

The Marginal Revolution is widely credited to the Austrian School economist Carl Menger (1840–1921) and his systematic book, *Principles of Economics* (1871), though its *subjectivist* and *marginalist* ideas were much older. As far back as 1776, the French philosopher Étienne Bonnet de Condillac (1714–80) had argued that value was not a physical quality of a thing, but a mark of how much it satisfied some human want. Writing in 1803, Jean-Baptiste Say reached much the same conclusion.

Then in 1826 the German economist Johann Heinrich von Thünen (1783–1850) began to develop *marginal productivity* theory. Producers would continue to hire workers, he reasoned, until the extra yield produced by the last (*marginal*) worker diminished to no more than the employer was willing to pay them. This *marginal yield*, therefore, determined the wage rate and the number of people who would be employed. And what was true for *labour* would be true of *capital* inputs too: producers would continue to pay for capital equipment until the additional output it produced (its *marginal output*) diminished to equal the cost of installing, running and maintaining it.

Two years on, the English lawyer and economist Nassau William Senior (1790–1864) saw *scarcity* as the most important factor in determining value. Goods that had *value* (i.e. *economic* goods like food or clothing) were necessarily *scarce* ones. Goods that were *abundant* (i.e. *free* goods such as air) had no value. Senior also worked on the *diminishing marginal utility* idea, as did the German economist Hermann Heinrich Gossen (1810–58). Gossen asked how consumers would select the *combination* of goods that, within their budgets, would *maximise their total satisfaction*. He concluded that they would strive to acquire different goods until the *last units* of each good they acquired gave them equal satisfaction (*utility*).

In 1871, the same year as Menger's *Principles* was published, the English economist and logician William Stanley Jevons (1835–82) published *The Theory of Political Economy*, which weaves these early ideas into a systematic, *subjectivist* theory of value. To him, *utility* was the power of a thing to produce pleasure or prevent pain for its consumer; *value* was the *relationship* between the object and the individual's utility. But this was, he observed, a 'somewhat novel opinion' given the labour theory's dominance up to then.

The Neoclassical School

The Neoclassical School economists emerged in the late nineteenth and early twentieth centuries, building on both Classical and Marginalist foundations. They adopted the scientific approach of the Classical School, but their focus was less on total production, more on how consumers gain satisfaction from products, and thus on how they choose them and exchange them. They accepted that value was *subjective*, not a matter of production costs. (People dive for pearls, for example, because they are valued; pearls are not valued because people dive for them.) And the Neoclassical economists applied *marginalist* analysis to their analyses.

They believed that land, capital and labour all contribute to value. But they did not share the Classical (nor Marxist) view of society as fixed, opposing social classes rooted in these different factors of production. They saw a society in which *rational*, classless *economic agents* with set preferences sought out the combination of resources and manufacturing processes that would maximise consumers' *utility* and businesses' *profit* within the limits of their budgets. And it was the *value created by the end product* (e.g. an omelette) that drove production (e.g. farming, transportation, restaurants), and determined the nature and value of the *production goods* (e.g. land, vehicles, kitchens) that would be committed to the production of that end product.

Relying heavily on mathematical methods and equations, the Neoclassical economists were able to construct very sophisticated theories. They showed how the markets for both consumer and capital goods might tend towards a balance (*equilibrium*) where supply equals demand; they explored the role of *consumer demand* in determining efficient resource use; and they developed a *theory of the firm* and its role in the economy.

This emphasis on supply and demand, marginal utility, market equilibrium and the use of mathematics is still characteristic of economics today.

Key figures of the Neoclassical School

Jevons and Menger provided the subjectivist and marginalist foundations for the Neoclassical School, but its leading figure would be Alfred Marshall (1842–1924), whose *Principles of Economics* (1890) blended these ideas into a cohesive system. He popularised *supply and demand curves* and explored how individual markets reach balance (*market equilibrium*) given the different sensitivities of supply and demand to price changes.

The Neoclassical approach allowed other thinkers to reach other powerful conclusions that still feature in economics textbooks today. Thus, Léon Walras (1834–1910) used mathematics to show the conditions under which *all* markets in an economy could come into *general equilibrium*. Vilfredo Pareto (1848–1923) outlined situations where it was impossible to reallocate available resources without making someone worse off – what we now call *Pareto Optimality*. John Bates Clark (1847–1938) used marginalist theory to explain how labour and capital markets affect wages and profits. Irving Fisher (1867–1947) contributed on monetary policy, interest rates and prices. Knut Wicksell (1851–1926) explored how interest rates affect price levels. And Arthur Pigou (1877–1959) analysed the overall welfare of society, introducing the idea of *externalities* such as pollution costs.

Alfred Marshall

Marshall saw supply and demand as 'the two blades of the scissors' that determine the quantities and prices of goods that are traded. Marginal utility analysis could explain the nature of consumers' *demand*, he observed; but the nature of producers' *supply* was important too. And he saw time and industrial organisation as key factors in that supply. Take the case where some event raises consumers' demand for a product (in today's world, perhaps the endorsement of a social media influencer). At first, says Marshall, that will raise the product's price because the available stocks are fixed. But then, seeing the increase in demand, producers will try to increase their supply of the product, drawing in more labour and other easily expanded inputs to do so. Prices might then moderate as a result. But it will take producers longer to build and install the new capital equipment (e.g. plant and machinery) needed to further increase their supply going forward. Only then might prices start to fall again.

While developing such thoughts, Marshall introduced other concepts that economists use today. One was the *elasticity of supply* – how much or how little producers respond to price changes by raising or lowering their supply; and the analogous *elasticity of demand* – how much or how little the demand from consumers rises or falls in response to falling or rising prices. Another concept was *consumer surplus,* where the value that a consumer puts on a good is greater to them than the value of what they pay for it. (And since the market price of each unit of the good is the same – one omelette in a restaurant is the same price as the next, for example – *diminishing marginal utility* means that this surplus will also diminish with each additional unit consumed.) Again, there is an analogous *producer surplus*, the difference between the market price that producers receive for each unit of a product and the minimum price that they would, in reality, be willing to accept. Marshall used such concepts to explore how various changes (e.g. tax cuts or rises) might affect the overall well-being of the community, known as *social welfare*.

Marshall sought to make economics a modern science that would offer a general explanation of how markets worked. Accordingly, he made his analysis *abstract*, a contrast to the *historical-political* approach of Adam Smith. But this meant that his investigations of market behaviour had to be based on many broad assumptions. He had to take much as 'given', such as the state of technology, market institutions and consumer preferences. He knew, of course, that real economic activity is never so static but evolves and adapts (something that later economists often forget). Yet his abstract reasoning enabled Marshall to develop a pure science that provided the foundations for economic thought over the next century.

Other significant contributions

The American inventor and economist Irving Fisher used Marshall's abstract Neoclassical approach to make important developments in the Classical *Quantity Theory of Money*. This is the idea that changes in the quantity of money in an economy (such as the notes and coins created by the authorities and the amount that people choose to hold in their bank accounts) will affect prices – and will do so proportionately. If the authorities print and circulate more banknotes, for instance, the Quantity Theory suggests that the prices of goods will rise in step. Fisher famously summarised this idea in the equation $MV = PT$. That is, the total amount of money in the economy, multiplied by its velocity (i.e. the frequency at which consumers and suppliers exchange it), equals the overall price level multiplied by the number of transactions made. He believed that, in the short run at least, the velocity of money and the number of transactions would be stable, so any change in the quantity of money would affect prices directly. Later *monetarist* economists from the Chicago School would build on this analysis.

With his book *The Theory of Interest* (1930) Fisher also provided a Neoclassical explanation of interest rates. These he saw as a balance between 'impatience' (people's desire to consume things now) and 'opportunity' (the prospect of producing and consuming more of those things in the future). He distinguished *nominal* from *real* interest rates, factoring in inflation, and showed how *nominal* interest rates would rise when people expected future inflation.

Many later Neoclassical economists concerned themselves with *welfare economics* – how to maximise economic benefits across the community. Pareto, as mentioned above, suggested that the allocation of goods across the community was *efficient* or *optimal* if you cannot change the allocation to make anyone *better off* without making someone else *worse off*. He also introduced *indifference curves* that show how people might trade off one good against another and remain equally satisfied with (i.e.

'indifferent' to) the new allocation. And he is further remembered for the *80:20 Rule* – originally an observation about land ownership but now extended into an economic rule of thumb. For example, it is said that 80 per cent of a firm's profits come from 20 per cent of its customers, or that 80 per cent of its business comes through 20 per cent of its advertising – even if firms rarely know which 20 per cent that is.

Also focusing on *welfare economics*, Arthur Pigou applied Neoclassical methods to the study of *externalities* – the costs (or benefits) of economic activity that affect other parties (e.g. the effects of a smoky factory chimney on local residents). He argued that to maximise the welfare of society in general, private incentives must become aligned with social outcomes. Accordingly, he proposed taxes (known as *Pigovian* taxes) and subsidies to curb harmful externalities and promote beneficial ones.

Pigou saw economic output as a measure of social welfare, suggesting policies to boost output while reducing the inequality of its distribution. He argued for progressive taxes to transfer income from rich to poor, using a *marginal utility* argument – that a high earner would value an extra pound or dollar of income much less than would a low earner.

Criticism and contemporary extension

While Neoclassical economics has been highly influential, it has faced criticism, particularly for the abstractness of its assumptions. Austrian School economists (chapter 8) reject its assumption of perfect competition, for example, while behavioural economists (chapter 10) question the assumption that economic agents behave rationally, pointing to phenomena such as the 'herd instinct' and market bubbles.

Yet the core principles and approaches of Neoclassical economics continue to shape modern economic analysis and still provide useful ways to understand how people and markets behave. Thus, Neoclassical approaches have helped to analyse the distribution of income, and to explain how taxes, subsidies and technological progress affect the relative earnings of labour and capital. They have provided insights into the potential welfare impacts of public policy changes. And they help explain the behaviour of imperfect but real-world markets.

Analysis of marginal costs and benefits, meanwhile, has been used to study a wide range of producer behaviours, including price discrimination, the effects of different market structures and the impact of government policies.

Despite its limitations, Neoclassical economics still shapes how economists analyse a wide range of economic issues, from producer behaviour and prices to the management of the economy as a whole (*macroeconomics*). It may not *fully explain* economic reality, but it still helps us to *understand* it.

6 KEYNES AND THE KEYNESIANS

Keynes's contribution

John Maynard Keynes was a British economist whose ideas had a deep and lasting impact on economic thought and policy from the 1920s to the 1970s. He turned the focus from the details of individual decisions, markets and prices (*microeconomics*) to the big picture of GDP, inflation and employment across the entire economy (*macroeconomics*). In doing so, he challenged the Classical and Neoclassical assumption that markets would automatically come into balance (*equilibrium*) and deliver maximum output and full employment. Instead, he thought these things would fluctuate depending on the total level of demand in the economy (*aggregate demand*), which in turn depended on several factors, including how much people chose to spend, save or invest.

But, he argued, government could compensate for fluctuations in these choices. Most importantly, it could correct economic downturns by raising its spending and cutting taxes, which would leave more money in people's pockets and so boost their demand, and by lowering interest rates, which would boost investment.

Such interventions, Keynes believed, would stabilise the economy and help achieve full and stable output and employment.

In the decades after World War II, this *macroeconomic* approach came to dominate economic thought and policy, contributing to the creation of the welfare state and the widespread use of tax and spending policies aimed at boosting output and employment.

Background to Keynes's ideas

The period leading up to Keynes's most significant work was turbulent. The effects of world war, then the experience of the Great Depression, still haunted the world economy. The theoretical abstractions of the Neoclassicals, with their confidence that markets automatically tend towards an equilibrium that maximises output and employment, seemed unable to explain the persistent unemployment, instability and stagnation that prevailed.

It seemed increasingly urgent for economists to address these problems, find solutions and maximise social welfare. Accordingly, their focus shifted away from abstract theorising and laissez-faire solutions, and towards questions of practical public policy and the potential role of government intervention. And this new approach was bolstered by the continuing development of better analytical techniques, including improved data collection and mathematical modelling.

Keynes's analysis and prescriptions

The General Theory

Keynes's *General Theory of Employment, Interest, and Money* (1936) spearheaded this new approach. It marked a pivotal moment in the evolution of economic thought and how economists engaged with practical public issues and policies. While the Classical and Neoclassical economists had focused on *how* production worked and was distributed, the *General Theory* focused on *maximising* that product and *stabilising* its growth.

By looking at *macroeconomic aggregates* such as the prevailing totals of income, consumption, saving and investment, Keynes concluded that what drove total (*aggregate*) investment and employment was the overall, *aggregate demand* for goods.

That in turn would depend on psychological factors, such as how much consumers chose to keep in *liquid assets* (such as cash) rather than put into savings or investments, what financial yield individuals and businesses thought their investments might generate, and how both consumers and producers would react when faced with risk and uncertainty. All these factors, thought Keynes, would affect what consumers were willing to spend, what investors were willing to lend, and what capital goods businesses would demand. But sometimes, these psychological factors could lead to spending, investment and employment decisions that were less than optimal – and so to weaker and less stable economic growth.

Keynes believed that in difficult economic times (such as those he was writing in), when demand and investment were low, the economy would not automatically correct itself but could settle into persistently high unemployment and low growth. Indeed, he thought, there would be a *multiplier* effect: a decrease in spending by any given amount would lead to a fall in economic output of even more. That was because, when consumer spending fell, firms would cut their production, so employment and wages would decline, and people's spending would fall further, setting off a downward spiral.

Macroeconomic policy

Earlier, in *A Tract on Monetary Reform* (1923), Keynes had focused on *monetary policy* as the way to stabilise the economy, by managing the *money supply* (the total quantity of money in existence, such as notes, coins and bank deposits), along with interest rates, to control inflation, currency fluctuations and investment levels. But after the Great Depression, he concluded that lowering interest rates or increasing the money supply would be insufficient to revive demand in an economy that had fallen into a *liquidity trap* – where prospects were so dire that people chose to hoard cash rather than spend or invest.

So, to offset falling demand and escape the trap, Keynes in the *General Theory* (1936) urged a much more interventionist strategy. The government, he advised, should use *fiscal policy* to add to the total (aggregate) demand in the economy by increasing its own spending (e.g. on welfare, infrastructure projects and other public programmes) and by cutting taxation, which would place, or leave, more spending power in the hands of consumers, businesses and investors. Now the multiplier would work positively. The extra consumer spending would prompt businesses to raise output, invest, expand employment and raise wages, causing spending and economic activity to spiral upwards. Such interventionist prescriptions were plainly a long way from the laissez-faire policies of the prevailing economic orthodoxies.

Influence

With World War II devastating world economies, Keynes's macroeconomic focus and interventionist policy prescriptions came to be seen as appropriate, necessary and urgent ways to deal with economic crises. They evolved into a mixed approach to economic management, with *monetary policy* to manage inflation and stabilise currencies, and *fiscal policy* to stabilise demand and address unemployment. Interest rates would be manipulated to influence investment and spending decisions. And governments would spend on public infrastructure, unemployment benefits and welfare programmes to boost employment and economic revival.

But while Keynes's policies were originally intended to deal with crises, stabilise activity and create more certain conditions for future growth, they quickly grew beyond these aims. They would be used in the hope of boosting growth that was merely sluggish, and of reaching 'full employment' targets that were often over-ambitious. And when things really were booming, politicians would see this as success and would be reluctant to use their policy tools to curb such 'overheating'. *Deficit spending*, where governments spent more than they raised in taxation, then became the norm. And much of that spending went into the creation and expansion of the welfare states that would continue to grow through the rest of the twentieth century.

Neo-Keynesians

Keynes's ideas were developed further by his followers. They subjected the macroeconomic aggregates to more advanced mathematical modelling, exploring the different short-run and long-run results of policy changes, and reaching abstract conclusions, including the 'Phillips Curve' idea that it was worth suffering a little inflation in order to reduce unemployment (a conclusion that the Chicago School economists would strongly contest).

In the 1960s, 'Neo-Keynesian' economists such as Alvin Hansen (1887–1975), Sir John Hicks (1904–89) and Paul Samuelson (1915–2009) began to explore how macroeconomic events could be affected by *microeconomic* factors such as prices, preferences, costs, technologies, risks and uncertainties. In more mathematical detail than Keynes had done, they showed how *rigidities* in prices, wages and other factors explained why markets did not automatically self-regulate. Such rigidities included the reluctance of workers (often led by their trade unions) to take pay cuts in response to falling demand, the impact of slowdowns on morale and thus on productivity, the power of monopolies to maintain high prices, and interest rates being held at rates that were no longer appropriate for current conditions.

This approach merged Keynes's macroeconomics with the Neoclassical microeconomics focus. It recognised the importance of market forces but retained a confidence in the ability of government to direct those forces toward the macroeconomic ideals of full employment, economic stability, growth and social welfare – a major extension of interventionist policies. Activist Neo-Keynesian fiscal policy, with deficit spending on government projects and welfare programmes, became the dominant economic strategy across many parts of the world.

Monetarist and other criticisms

By the 1970s and 1980s, however, the Neo-Keynesian orthodoxy was wearing thin. With the expansion in their size and activities, Western governments had become clumsy and bureaucratic. Critics noted that while politicians were happy to use expansionary policies to boost output and employment, they were reluctant to contract their spending when needed. Inflation became high, widespread and persistent, while unemployment and sluggish growth remained – the 'stagflation' that the orthodoxy found hard to explain.

Some economists, such as Milton Friedman (1912–2006) and others from the Chicago School, began to challenge this prevailing Keynesian orthodoxy. They argued that economies work best when markets operate freely, with minimal government intervention; that markets are inherently inefficient and self-regulating; that Keynesian interventionism distorted markets and reduced their efficiency; that deficit spending and borrowing was unsustainable; that excessive welfare spending undermined incentives; that over-expansive monetary policy produced only inflation; and that government spending crowded out more efficient private investment.

Further criticism of 'big government' interventionism came from the Austrian School (who had shown how inept expansionary policy produced damaging boom–bust cycles), from Behavioural Economics (which questioned the assumption that economic actors choose rationally), and by the Public Choice School (who observed how government policymaking and implementation was distorted by politics and self-interest).

Such assaults would undermine confidence in governments' ability to manage economies effectively or rationally. In time, they would prompt a reversal of the orthodox thinking and prescriptions, particularly in the US and Europe. New approaches would be based on open trade, market deregulation, balanced government budgets and monetary prudence – all aimed at creating the essential conditions for enterprise and growth, without governments having to lead it.

7 THE CHICAGO SCHOOL

The Chicago School of Economics is a distinctive strain of Neoclassical thought developed by scholars at (or associated with) the University of Chicago, most notably Frank Knight (1885–1972), Milton Friedman (1912–2006), George Stigler (1911–91) and Gary Becker (1930–2014) – the last three of whom became Nobel laureates.

Through most of the twentieth century, Chicago School scholars made significant contributions to economics, including microeconomics, rational expectations, human capital, monetary and fiscal policy, industrial organisation, public choice, and the relation between law and economics. Their work and approach continue to be influential today.

Principles

The Chicago School is distinguished by several strong characteristics.

First is the belief that individuals and firms are rational: individuals seek to maximise their utility, and firms their profit. People respond predictably to incentives, such as changes in the costs they face. Indeed, they do this across many aspects of life – family, education, even crime. And because markets are driven by rational actors, they allocate resources efficiently without needing government intervention.

All this gives Chicago economists their second characteristic, a strong faith in free markets. They accept that markets are often imperfect, but see many of those imperfections stemming from, or worsened by, government controls and regulations. At the microeconomic level, intervening in markets stops those markets from working properly, leading to unintended and harmful results. And at the broader level, the time it takes to collect and analyse the macroeconomic data, then to plan and execute the policies based on it, creates problems too. For instance, by the time a Neo-Keynesian policy aimed at correcting a downswing comes into effect, economic activity may well have turned already into an upswing (and vice versa): so instead of promoting stability, the effect can be to make upswings and downswings *worse*. Chicago scholars therefore urge governments to limit themselves to *creating the right conditions for enterprise and growth* only. Such thinking informed many political movements including the 1980s governments of Margaret Thatcher in the UK and Ronald Reagan in the US.

Third, Chicago scholars (notably Gary Becker) believe that the ideas of rationality and efficiency can explain not just economic outcomes but other parts of social life. Becker, for example, saw *criminal action* as a rational choice between costs (e.g. detection and punishment) and benefits (e.g. the proceeds of theft). This has helped inform governments' anti-crime strategies. Likewise, migration, childbearing, and much else can be analysed in rational choice terms, with people weighing benefits (e.g. the joy derived from children) against costs (e.g. the commitment and time that child-raising requires). This approach reveals that many social actions which seem irrational are in fact very rational.

A fourth characteristic is the Chicago economists' empirical rigour and use of data. For example, they confirm their belief that individuals and firms are rational by observing how people respond to incentives, such as price changes, in the real world; and they rely greatly on econometrics and statistical techniques. Thus, Chicago scholars used crime and family statistics to test Becker's social economic concepts; Stigler used empirical studies to confirm how consumers use information; and Friedman compiled very large amounts of data to back his money-supply explanation of the Great Depression.

Another hallmark of the Chicago School, associated particularly with Milton Friedman, is *monetarism*, the idea that the supply of money (notes, coins, bank account balances, etc.) in the economy is the main driver of inflation – with 'too much money chasing too few goods'. Once more, this analysis suggests that governments should reject interventionist monetary policy and instead aim to set long-term rules to keep the quantity of money in line with output; again, it is based heavily on empirical measures; and yet again it has influenced governments, leading to a sharp decline in world inflation over the last quarter of the twentieth century.

Indeed, the Chicago School's interest in and relevance to public policy is another defining characteristic. Chicago analyses have provided the foundation for policy in many areas, such as the inflation control and crime deterrence measures already mentioned. They have also influenced deregulation policies (which Stigler showed were costly and were often captured by producer interests), taxation (with lower taxes demonstrated to reduce distortion and raise incentives), education (with education and training seen as an investment in people's productive capacity), and much more.

Origins

After its foundation in 1890, the University of Chicago soon became a centre for economic thought and research. Influential economists associated with it included John Dewey (1859–1952), Thorstein Veblen (1857–1929) and Jacob Viner (1892–1970), who all laid the groundwork for the Chicago School's emphasis on empirical analysis. But it was Frank Knight, who joined the University in 1927, who shaped the School's later approach.

Focusing on real-world economics, Knight stressed the vital role of entrepreneurs in driving economic progress in a world of *risk* (which was measurable) and *uncertainty* (which was not). He saw *uncertainty* as a particularly important factor in entrepreneurial decisions. To him, the Neoclassical assumptions – perfect competition and perfectly informed firms maximising their profits in a known world – concealed everything that was important in economics. With risk and uncertainty all around, individuals and firms could never be perfectly informed. They had to collect, analyse and act on whatever information they could glean, and they faced the *information costs* of all that. They faced *transaction costs* too, the everyday expenses of simply bringing goods to market and trading them.

But it was Knight's pupil Milton Friedman who emerged as the most influential figure of the Chicago School. An accomplished scholar and able communicator, his criticism of Neo-Keynesian economic policies and his robust advocacy of free markets helped solidify Chicago's reputation. His insights would be critical in driving economic reform in the UK, Eastern Europe and Latin America. But it was *monetarism* that would make his reputation.

Monetarism

Together with the microeconomist George Stigler, Friedman argued that regulations and other interventions often created market distortions that led to further unintended problems. Their work in demonstrating the superiority of free markets with minimal regulation (e.g. in the market for rentable accommodation) provided the intellectual basis for the wide-scale political movement towards deregulation and privatisation in the 1980s and 1990s, particularly in the UK, the US and former Soviet countries.

Due largely to Friedman, the Chicago School's strong endorsement of *monetarism* would pose a direct challenge to the Neo-Keynesian orthodoxy. While the Keynesians prescribed expansionary fiscal and monetary policy to boost output during a downturn, Friedman argued that the main long-term effect of this would not be growth, but inflation.

He reached this conclusion after reviving and reinterpreting the *Quantity Theory of Money*, an idea that Neo-Keynesianism had left for dead. As mentioned, the Quantity Theory maintained that the level of prices depended mainly on the total quantity of money in existence, such as coins, banknotes and balances in bank accounts. Friedman produced many real-world examples to support this view. But his version of the theory would help explain why inflation had become so pervasive and so hard to eliminate.

One reason, he argued, was the different short- and long-term effects of changes in the quantity of money. A monetary expansion might well stimulate output, as its advocates hoped; but that effect would be only *temporary*. Over the long term, the expansion would only raise prices, i.e. create inflation. That is because an expansion in the money supply means that individuals and firms find that they now have more money available to spend and invest. So at first, business booms. But, just like people getting habituated to a drug such that larger and larger doses are needed for it to deliver a stimulus, so everyone gets used to the extra money in circulation and only larger and larger expansions of it will keep the boom going. The only long-term effect is that the additional money bids up prices, i.e. causes *inflation*.

Friedman, however, thought things were even worse than this. His empirical work had shown that the *lags* between changes to the money supply and their effects on prices and output were *long* and *variable*. In a downturn, for example, it would take the authorities time to recognise the situation, agree that a stimulus was needed, decide on an expansionary policy and put that policy into effect. It would then take time for the extra money to enter the economy and for the public to react (e.g. by spending more or ordering and installing extra productive capacity) and for those actions to have their effect on output. By the time the policy has had its effect, therefore, things might already have recovered, and the authorities could find that they are expanding into an upturn, the opposite of their intentions.

Monetary policy, Friedman concluded, was far too blunt a tool for this sort of Neo-Keynesian 'fine tuning'. He argued instead for a *monetary rule* – a set target for steady and predictable growth in the money supply, broadly matching the long-term growth of output – as a much more effective way of keeping prices stable.

Unsurprisingly, these conclusions were resisted by orthodox thinkers. But Friedman's authoritative 1963 publication, with co-author Anna Schwartz, of *A Monetary History of the United States* forced them to reconsider. Until then, Keynesians blamed the 1930s Great Depression on market failures such as a collapse in consumption or investment. But Friedman and Schwartz showed in detail how it had been the monetary authorities who were at fault: they had turned a stock market crash into a depression by letting the money supply shrink by over a *third*. There were many reasons why this happened: the authorities' desire to curb speculation, their underestimation of the crisis, their fear of inflation, their failure to support failing banks, their focus on preserving gold reserves rather than economic stability, and more. But, whatever the reasons, it was a record-breaking 'Great Contraction' as Friedman and Schwartz called it, with profound depressive effects. This was a radical reinterpretation of the Great Depression, and it reinvigorated the support for monetarism.

By the 1970s, people were losing faith in the Keynesian prescriptions, which seemed to bring only high inflation and low growth. Friedman's view gained further ground, and central banks began to adopt more conservative monetary policies. But these proved difficult to put into practice. There were many possible definitions of the *money supply*, so it was hard to know which *forms* of money should be included and controlled; and of course the policy would be ineffective if markets used types of money that were not controlled.

Eventually, therefore, though contrary to Friedman's recommendations, central banks came to focus on *interest rates* as a way of controlling the *demand* for money (and loans) rather than trying to control its *supply*. But the end target was the same, and the new era of more sober monetary policy brought a significant fall in inflation across the globe.

Rational Expectations Theory

Another area in which the Chicago School was important, stemming from their belief in the rationality of individuals, firms and markets, was the development of *rational expectations theory*.

If we are to predict how economic events might unfold, we must understand how individuals and businesses form their future plans. Keynes thought that people make systematic mistakes in their planning because they tend to assume that the future will be much like the past. That means they fail to predict changing conditions and are then slow to adjust to events. Such errors mean that markets do not balance, with unwelcome results. For example, if workers fail to anticipate a sudden rise in prices, and have not demanded higher wages to compensate, they will find themselves worse off.

Friedman, though, believed that people were shrewder than this. In *A Theory of the Consumption Function* (1957) he suggested that, while people do base their expectations on past experience, they update those expectations when they no longer match reality. For instance, if prices surge, people will revise their expectations of future price rises upward and will adapt their spending plans accordingly. Likewise, families plan their spending on the basis of what they expect their *lifetime* earnings to be, not just their *current* earnings, and they revise those plans if their prospects change. This approach became known as *adaptive expectations* theory.

A more general, abstract approach was posited by the (non-Chicago) economist John Muth (1930–2005) but was developed by Robert Lucas (1937–2013) at Chicago, thereby becoming strongly associated with the Chicago School. This approach holds that individuals and firms understand how the economy functions; they base their future expectations on the relevant information that is available to them; they process that information objectively; and they learn from their past mistakes. This became known as *rational expectations theory*.

In terms of business, the theory suggests that asset prices, such as stock market prices, reflect all the available information about a company's future prospects. New information will be incorporated quickly into the prices that investors are willing to pay, making it hard for anyone to beat the market.

The theory also has important implications for policymakers. If economic agents are indeed able to anticipate with some accuracy the effects of policy changes, the intended effect of those policies might be undermined. For example, if the government raises its spending to boost demand, consumers and investors may conclude that the resulting budget shortfall will soon have to be covered by tax rises. They might then prepare for that extra cost by reining in their spending and postponing investment – the opposite of what the policy intended to achieve.

Unsurprisingly, therefore, policymakers and government economists have needed to take rational expectations theory seriously and have been significantly influenced by it in their policymaking and modelling.

Human Capital Theory

Another way in which Chicago scholars, particularly Gary Becker (1930–2014), contributed to the analysis of human economic behaviour was the development of *human capital theory*. This regards an individual's knowledge, skills and fitness as a form of *capital* that can be invested in and accumulated. Such investment includes education, training, on-the-job learning, even health, nutrition, fitness and other lifestyle choices.

Investments in an individual's *human capital* can increase their future productivity and earnings, just as investments in physical capital goods can do for producers. Thus, studies show that individuals with higher levels of education, such as a degree or a vocational training qualification, tend to earn higher lifetime incomes compared to those without. Because education and training increase people's knowledge and skills, they become more productive and more employable as workers.

The human capital idea can be applied to a variety of human situations. For instance, it helps explain household decisions, such as parents' huge devotion of time and resources to their children's upbringing, education and health. The theory suggests that it is perfectly rational for parents to make these costly investments, believing that they will bring their children future benefit. (Successful people whose parents forced them to do their homework would probably agree.)

Policy guidance

As well as being a significant contribution to understanding aspects of human behaviour, human capital theory also provides a guide for public policy. Though individuals can and do invest in their own human capital, community programmes such as the provision of schools, local fitness clubs and youth groups can also contribute. And while most of the benefits of human capital investment accrue to the individuals themselves, there may also be wider social benefits (such as the social benefit and productivity gains from having a skilled workforce).

Instead of governments viewing education, training, healthcare and other services simply as *costs*, therefore, the human capital idea encourages them to consider these programmes as *investments* that may yield wider benefits. This has prompted policies such as giving tax breaks for apprenticeship and vocational courses, improving access to lifelong learning, and encouraging positive health and fitness activities.

Supply-Side Economics

Stemming from their belief that individuals and firms respond rationally to incentives, the Chicago School made other significant contributions to the development and promotion of *supply-side economics*. This gained prominence in the 1980s and led to renewed focus on the effects of changes in tax rates and government policies on people's economic decisions and the economic effects that those decisions produced.

While Keynesian policies focused mainly on influencing *demand*, for example, Chicago economists argued that these interventions (especially tax rises) created *disincentives* against investment, work and entrepreneurship, which hampered economic growth. They instead advocated *supply-side* policies, such as reducing marginal tax rates and deregulating industries. They argued that these measures would stimulate economic growth by increasing the incentives for investment and enterprise.

Another example of supply-side thinking is the *Laffer Curve*, attributed to Chicago scholar Arthur Laffer (1940–), who developed it in the 1970s (though the idea is many centuries older). This represents the relationship between tax rates and revenues in a humpback graph. It suggests that when tax rates are raised, from zero upwards, the revenues they generate initially increase; but that, after a certain point, revenues will decrease again.

For example, a tax rate of 0 per cent would raise no revenue; then at higher rates, more and more individuals and businesses would be paying tax and so generating revenue for the government. But very high rates would discourage work and enterprise, since people would see less and less point in working or running a business when a large part of their earnings was being taxed away. Taxable activities would then decrease in volume (in economic parlance, the tax base would shrink) and the higher rates would deliver the government *less* revenue.

The exact point at which further tax increases will produce lower revenue is difficult to determine. It may depend on local circumstances, such as what tax levels people are used to, and other economic and political factors at the time. But the general principle seems to fit the empirical facts. For illustration, there have been several occasions when governments have significantly reduced their higher rates of income tax. It happened under the US presidencies of Calvin Coolidge in the 1920s, John F. Kennedy in the 1960s, Ronald Reagan in the 1980s and George W. Bush in the 2000s, as well as in Margaret Thatcher's UK administration in the 1980s. In each case, the share of tax revenue paid by the highest earners *increased* after the cut in tax rates.

Criticisms

A common criticism of Chicago economics is that markets are often less perfect than it supposes – as evidenced by bubbles, crashes, pollution and more. But the School would reply that markets, though imperfect, are still better than government alternatives, given the latter's bureaucracy, vested interests and corruption; and that many of the problems (such as bubbles and crashes) are the results of bad policy or (e.g. in the case of externalities) inadequate property rights. Thus, they largely blame the 2008 financial crisis on policy distortions such as housing subsidies, loose monetary policy and inept banking regulation.

Another objection is that Chicago free-market policies increase economic inequality. Chicago economists respond that inequality is a byproduct of rewarding productivity and innovation, but that those things drive economic growth, benefiting everyone. Nor are they deaf to hardship: Friedman, for example, proposed a *negative income tax* that could relieve poverty without distorting incentives.

Other critics say that monetary policy is not enough to manage the economy, and that other interventions are still needed. But Chicago monetarists argue that the evidence for monetary causes behind inflations and recessions is clear, and that fiscal policy (such as increased government spending) is too often motivated by politics rather than economics.

More superficially, Chicago economists – more precisely, their Chilean offshoot, the 'Chicago Boys' – were attacked for their involvement in the government of General Pinochet in Chile. But those Chilean economists respond that, whatever the *political* flaws of that regime, their involvement was limited to *economic* issues – and that they were successful in terms of reducing inflation, balancing budgets and boosting entrepreneurship and growth.

Conclusion

What most typifies the Chicago School is perhaps its application of pure economic theory, with a renewed emphasis on the importance of incentives, to a wide range of human activities. That includes not just work, enterprise, saving and investment but also family structure, migration, discrimination, education and more. This can (and does) provide important guidance for public policy. Becker's analysis of incentives in criminal behaviour, for example, concludes that crime-reduction policy should focus not on long punishments but on better policing and a speedy judicial process.

Chicago economists know that there is more to human choices than pure economics. The decision to work, or change job, start a business, raise a family, buy or rent a house, emigrate or stay, continue working or retire – all these depend heavily on individual emotions and character traits such as ambition, confidence, foresight, energy, love, family values, upbringing, culture and more.

And yet, all conscious human decisions *do* have at least some economic dimension. They involve individuals weighing in their minds the potential gains and losses of their actions, just as investors would weigh up potential costs and returns. While Chicago School reasoning may seem abstract, its conclusions are supported by rigorous empirical testing. So its influence, not only on economic enquiry but on public policy formation, should come as no surprise.

8 THE AUSTRIAN SCHOOL

The Austrian School of Economics is difficult to place chronologically among the different schools of thought because it has existed so long and developed in so many ways. It goes back to the marginalism and subjectivism of Carl Menger, which informed the Neoclassical School and then the Chicago School. But Austrian economists would critique the abstract methods of both. The Austrian School rose in importance for its early-twentieth-century work on money, capital and business cycles and the debate on economic calculation under socialism. It provided the main criticism of Keynes and his followers, though it was eclipsed by their apparent success. More recently, its focus on the psychology of economic choice has informed the Public Choice School and Behavioural Economics. It has also contributed to information science and shown why even the most sophisticated initiatives of modern economists are inevitably short of the vital facts needed to make them work.

Origin and principles

The Austrian School is characterised by its *subjectivism* and *marginalism,* its *focus on the individual* as the starting point for economic analysis, its *critique of central planning*, its explanation of *how markets process information*, its stress on the importance of *time and capital* in the structure of production, its emphasis on the dynamism of markets, and its support for *minimal government intervention*.

Menger's book *Principles of Economics* (1871) marks the foundation of the Austrian approach. Menger rejected the Classical focus on labour costs as the determinant of value, emphasising instead the *subjective* nature of value and the *marginal* value derived from additional quantities of a good (though he did not himself use the word *margin* – that would be introduced by later Austrian economists).

The Austrian School, whose prominent members also included Friedrich von Wieser (1851–1926), Eugen von Böhm-Bawerk (1851–1914), Ludwig von Mises (1881–1973) and Friedrich Hayek (1899–1992), rejected the idea that economic analysis can be reduced to *macroeconomic* totals such as *aggregate demand* or *aggregate employment*. They argued that these totals mix together things that are quite heterogeneous and conceal the motives and choices of individual human beings, which are what really drive economic events. There could be no meaningful causal relationships between statistical *aggregates*. Instead, economic analysis must start from the aims and actions of individuals, each with their own ambitions, purposes and preferences – an approach known as *methodological individualism* – and deduce its conclusions logically from that.

In contrast to the Neoclassical focus on *equilibrium*, Austrians see economic life as *dynamic* – a continuous process of discovery, entrepreneurship, innovation and change. Consumer tastes, technologies and the availability of resources are never static; nor are prices, which reflect all of those changing things and more. And the need to keep responding to change is what makes *entrepreneurship* so important (and restrictions on innovation so damaging). Production also takes *time*, during which conditions can change, causing losses as past investments prove inappropriate. Such thinking underpins the distinctive Austrian theory of *trade cycles*.

Given the dynamic nature of economic life, Austrians rejected the contemporary enthusiasm for central economic planning. While conscious planning might sound like a good idea, they argued that it could never perform better than markets. Thus in 1920, Mises raised the *socialist calculation problem*, the idea that without market prices, which signal where there are gluts and shortages, central planners can never make efficient choices about what should be produced and the most cost-effective ways to produce and distribute those things. That shortcoming would lead to very wasteful investment decisions (as borne out by Soviet socialism over the next decades).

But how is society organised if it is not planned? Hayek pointed out that many human institutions (e.g. language and markets) are actually *self-organising systems* – what he called *spontaneous orders*. These evolve naturally and operate efficiently without needing any conscious control. Thus markets, through their price system, manage vast amounts of dispersed, personal and partial information – details that no planner could ever collect or process.

Because the Austrian approach emphasises individual choices, dispersed information, the limits of central planning and the need to innovate freely, they take the view that markets coordinate human activity far better than governments can do. Indeed, they argue that government intervention, by distorting markets, prices and trade, can seriously destabilise the delicate, evolved economic system.

It is useful to look at some of these principles in more detail.

Subjectivism versus Keynesianism

The subjectivist explanation of value has been mentioned earlier, but it is worth revisiting because, despite its diverse origins, it is now associated centrally with the Austrian School and informs all their work.

Following Menger, Austrians see *value* not as an *objective* quality (like weight or density), but as the *subjective* assessments (i.e. the personal judgements) of the individuals concerned. And, of course, different people value things differently. Comic book collectors, for example, might dream of owning editions containing the first appearances of Superman or Spider-Man, while other people might see no value in them at all.

The same is true of *costs*. These are not objective either, but a matter of how an individual values them. Thus one person might think a rare Spider-Man comic well worth its large asking price, while another might be unwilling to pay such an amount. Or, looking more broadly at how people value *non-financial* costs, one person might think the view from the top of a hill is not worth the effort of climbing it, while another might even think that the climb is part of the enjoyment.

Such human values cannot be put into statistics, the Austrians insist. We cannot average out one person's joy, for example, against another's distress. And people's valuations of things *change*. New technologies may deliver people greater satisfaction, leading them to abandon the old products they once valued. A celebrity endorsement or clever marketing strategy may make people value a product more than they did before. Fashions in clothes, haircuts, music, food, cars, pets and much else come, go and sometimes come back again. Economic life is *dynamic*.

Therefore, say Austrians, Keynesian-style aggregates and Neoclassical-style mathematics merely *obscure* everything that economics has to deal with – the diversity of human values, the large and dynamic array of choices people face and of the decisions they make, the complex ways their individual choices and actions affect and interact with others, and much else. Instead, they conclude, economic analysis should focus on understanding *how* individuals make decisions, and the role of economic factors in shaping them.

Time, uncertainty and ignorance

Not only are economic processes *dynamic*: the *time* taken for them to work out, the risk involved and the *uncertainty* of how they will work out, all affect how people choose to spend or invest, and therefore the economic outcomes that result.

In Neoclassical economics, and most textbooks today, time is not mentioned as a relevant factor or is regarded as having little or no effect on outcomes. To Austrians, however, *time is a key factor* in human decision-making and is a major factor in shaping economic outcomes.

Imperfect knowledge

Time is critical, say the Austrians, because individuals make decisions and formulate their plans within the context of a *future* that is uncertain and a *present* that they do not *fully* know. We might *think* we know all about our own economic situation, but in reality, none of us can possibly know all the countless factors that have shaped it and will continue to shape it. With billions of interconnected individuals constantly acting on their own assessments, priorities and preferences, economic life is far too complicated for that. And predicting precisely how events might turn out in the future, and how any action of ours will affect them, is even more impossible.

People make their choices, therefore, based on *imperfect knowledge* of the present and their personal, *subjective expectations* about what the future might hold. So, not surprisingly, they make mistakes. For instance, an entrepreneur might overestimate the public's demand for some good or service, and so waste resources on setting up a business that does not attract enough custom to succeed. Or they might fail to anticipate future tax rises that will eat into the viability of their enterprise. Or a competitor might suddenly invent a superior product. Or the price of a vital input might shoot up for some reason. And countless other possibilities might occur.

The lack of complete information about present and future circumstances inevitably leads people into errors, which might create losses and even force them to close their businesses and write off their investments. Even if their predictions prove broadly correct, they will still need to adjust to events along the way. This is no Neoclassical textbook-style smooth and automatic progression towards equilibrium but rather a stumbling process of trial and (unavoidable but often costly) error.

The importance of time and capital structure

Austrians see production as involving a network of processes that take different amounts of *time*. And they see the various capital goods that go into that production as part of a complex *capital structure*, all of which has to work together to create the final product. The more time and larger number of operations that the manufacturing process involves – in their words, the more *roundabout* the production – the more will it be affected by changing events, and the more numerous will be the opportunities for miscalculations and mistakes.

Even a simple product such as a loaf of bread, for example, requires advance planning. Land must be ploughed, but to produce the ploughs, metal ore must first be smelted and cast. Tractors to pull those ploughs must be manufactured, and the machine tools needed for that must themselves be manufactured. And all this even before a seed is planted. Later, the grain must be harvested and threshed, using yet other machines, and the grain then ground in mills and baked in ovens, which similarly must be created beforehand. So, the 'roundabout' production of something as simple as a loaf of bread requires an extensive chain of capital goods, and capital goods that produce those capital goods, and so on – a web of increasingly 'higher-order' capital goods, all of which must work together. But that intricate arrangement can easily go wrong.

Theory of the trade cycle

Hayek and Mises would develop the theory of time and capital to come up with a distinctive Austrian *theory of the trade cycle.*

Trade cycles are the up and down cycles in business activity that were very evident at the time – with depression in the 1870s, recovery in the 1880s, downturn again in the 1890s, rebound in the 1900s, another contraction soon after, the Roaring Twenties, then the Great Depression of the 1930s. Neoclassical economics, believing that markets would tend towards balance, struggled to explain these cycles, blaming them on external shocks, while Keynes would blame them on 'herd instinct' panics by investors.

Hayek and Mises, however, demonstrated that trade cycles were created by the inept monetary and credit policies of government central banks which disrupted the delicate and time-dependent structure of production. The desire of the authorities to boost economic activity, they explained, leads them to set interest rates below market levels. Those low rates allow producers to borrow more for investment and expansion. They induce consumers to borrow more too, allowing them to make more purchases, particularly of luxuries and larger purchases like homes, holidays or cars.

But with interest rates now set below market levels, the balance of saving and borrowing is disrupted. Borrowing booms because it is now cheaper, but savers become more reluctant to save because their savings earn so little interest. Soon, the amount that producers want to borrow from the banks (and other financial institutions) outstrips the amount that other people are willing to save into them. With the demand for loanable funds outstripping their supply, the banks have to cut back on their lending. They might even demand that borrowers repay their loans earlier than expected.

Businesses will then find themselves committed to investment projects, such as new factories and equipment or staff recruitment and training programmes, that are only part completed and can now no longer be funded. Projects will have to be abandoned, and workers laid off, all at great financial, social and personal cost. Painful readjustment will be necessary before things return to stability. The net result of the authorities' attempts to boost output is merely a bubble – a temporary artificial boom, which then collapses into a real and costly slump.

Doubts on interventionism

The coordinating power of markets

Trade cycles, time and capital theory, the follies of aggregation, subjectivism, and the inescapable limits to human knowledge, all make Austrians sceptical about the ambitions of interventionists and planners. Indeed, they believe that such activities will distort price signals and incentives and so do more harm than good. Instead, they advise, governments should set the *conditions* in which markets can operate efficiently (such as stable monetary policy, low taxes and open competition) and then allow free markets to do their job – which is to *coordinate* individuals' different economic plans, preferences, decisions and choices.

Austrians maintain that markets are remarkably effective at this *coordination* of economic activity. Prices are signals that convey to market participants the relative scarcity or plenty of goods and services, encapsulating huge amounts of dispersed information about all of their wants and plans. That allows investors, producers, workers and consumers to make informed choices about where their time, energy, effort and resources are best employed to generate the highest value, and for those different plans to be reconciled and coordinated.

The science of exchange

For these reasons, Austrians think it wrong to talk of 'the economy' as if it were a *machine* with some overall purpose. Rather, markets *evolve spontaneously* because they coordinate the actions of thousands, millions or perhaps billions of diverse individuals, each with their own different values, ambitions and purposes. And they do this without needing any central authority but by an automatic process of people adjusting their own plans to the actions of others.

A better word than *economy* for all this, say Austrians, would be *catallaxy*. (The word derives from the Greek for 'exchange' and was popularised by Mises, though it was originally coined much earlier.) The science of exchange and how markets coordinate exchange activity they call *catallactics*. And they prefer these terms because, unlike 'the economy', they do not imply that economic life works like a machine created for some common purpose.

Praxeology

A strong tradition in Austrian economics, popularised by Mises in his book *Human Action* (1949), is that much (possibly all) of importance about economic life can be derived, like mathematics, from self-evident axioms. From our own experience and that of those around us, for example, it is *self-evident* that humans have ambitions and goals. And to achieve these *ends*, they employ a variety of *means*. For instance, they want to feed themselves and their families; and to achieve this *end* they will employ the *means* of growing crops – or, more probably these days, of getting a job that allows them to pay for crops grown by others. Mises called the study of this goal-driven action *praxeology*.

From such simple premises, said Mises, a great deal of useful economic knowledge can be deduced. For example, the *ends* must be *valuable* to the person involved. The use of *means* suggests that the person has some *technical knowledge* of how to *achieve* those ends. We can deduce also that the satisfaction of those ends must take some *time* – otherwise, the person would have secured them already. In addition, we can deduce that the person believes that their actions will *make a difference* – otherwise there would be no point to them. We can also deduce that the relevant means are *scarce* – again, if they were free and plentiful, people would have already attained their ends. And with further reasoning, we can derive a wide range of other insights about values, supply, demand, prices, incentives, exchange, markets and the coordination of different people's goals and efforts in the pursuit of their individual ends.

Criticisms and responses

Mainstream economists complain that the Austrian methodology is too abstract and deductive, resting on inner feelings that cannot be measured or tested scientifically, making it useless for the scientific study of important economic issues such as the timing and severity of downturns. Indeed, say the critics, the Austrians' focus on individual action leads them to neglect (or even dismiss) trends in important macroeconomic measures, such as employment and inflation, which Keynesian and Neoclassical approaches highlight. And while the Austrian emphasis on subjective value has been influential, many economists think it insufficient to explain fully how markets operate – a task that would require a broader analysis of many more factors.

Also, critics note that Austrian economists often reject mathematical modelling, which (they say) makes their work less rigorous and less useful for policy analysis, since it denies them useful analytical tools. And because Austrians tend to support minimal government intervention (the critics continue), they have little to say on vital issues such as income inequality or externalities (e.g. pollution) where government action is needed.

In their defence, Austrians themselves recognise the limitations of the deductive method. Hayek, for example, argued that as well as what he called the *pure logic of choice*, we also need to examine the *situational* logic – such as the laws, political structures, customs and property rules within which individuals make their choices.

The bad news for the mainstream critics, however, is that even if economics *is* a genuine science, such complexities make it an inevitably inexact one. An analogy is the tides, which are the predictable result of gravitational forces. But whether a boat can sail at low tide or not is limited by the design of the harbour; and likewise, people's economic choices are limited by the design of the relevant institutions. And just as the tides influence whether a holidaymaker goes swimming or stays on dry land, so does context influence the economic decisions that people make. But even so, different individuals will make different choices. We cannot predict precisely what they will be; human beings are complex and unpredictable creatures.

The fruitfulness of Austrian insights

Most economists believe that their role is to predict and shape future economic events. By denying this as even possible, Austrians placed themselves outside the mainstream. But many of their core ideas about choice, their scepticism about government and their faith in the power of decentralised market processes still resonate widely today.

In a complex world of global supply chains and markets, for instance, governments clearly struggle to control decentralised processes that seem to work perfectly well without them. Meanwhile, their interventions rarely seem to deliver the advertised benefits. Commentators increasingly question the benefits of regulations, taxes, stimulus packages, and other policies. And the rise of crypto markets reflects the public's lack of faith in central banks and their ability to deliver sound money.

These are all Austrian themes. And in recent years, scholars have widened the range of Austrian thinking still further. For example, they have explored the role and importance of entrepreneurship, the dynamic nature of competition and the effects of risk, uncertainty, time, institutions, ethics, incentives and limited knowledge on economic decision making – all things that are underplayed in the mainstream textbooks, but which are important to our understanding of economic life.

Remember, too, that Menger's subjectivism and marginal analysis soon became an integral part of mainstream economics. And after some decades of being sidelined, other Austrian ideas and principles are now, increasingly, being integrated into contemporary economic thought.

9 THE PUBLIC CHOICE SCHOOL

The Public Choice School marks another break with Neo-classical and Neo-Keynesian thinking. To Public Choice scholars, governments are not angelic and benevolent public servants who can be relied on to intervene rationally in economic affairs. They are self-interested, just as economic actors are. Politicians chase fame and votes, bureaucrats pursue power and budgets, and influential interest groups put their own benefit ahead of the wider public's.

Economists who imagine that their policy proposals will be executed faithfully by the political system are over-optimistic, therefore. Government action may end up making things even worse than before.

The Public Choice School reaches such conclusions by applying the same tools that economists use to analyse economic choices – concepts such as cost, benefit, profit, loss, self-interest and so on – to political choices. The results are troubling to those who assume the rationality and impartiality of governments; so much so that Public Choice scholars argue for strong *constitutional restraints* to keep political self-interest in check.

Origins

Neo-Keynesians had great confidence that, with governments as their partners, they could manage economies – smoothing cycles, stabilising growth and boosting social welfare. But other economists who coalesced into the Public Choice School began to question these assumptions. They thought that governments could not be relied on to act dispassionately and efficiently; and that their interventions could therefore prove deficient or even destructive.

Ironically, as mentioned above, they reached this conclusion by applying the economics profession's own analytical tools to the policymaking process – which revealed systematic faults in its operation. While economists thought *market failure* required government interventions, they had overlooked that there was *government failure* too.

The Public Choice School had its roots in the 1940s but came to prominence in the 1960s and 1970s, a time of government expansion. It had a large influence on politicians in the 1980s and remains significant today.

An example of the School's thinking was the book *Democracy in Deficit: The Political Legacy of Lord Keynes*, by James Buchanan and Richard Wagner (1977). Neo-Keynesianism was damaging, they concluded, because politicians and officials inevitably distorted its policies. Politicians, for example, focus on creating vote-winning booms rather than on curbing over-expansion and balancing their budgets. Deficit spending then becomes the norm, budget restraint disappears and borrowing spirals upwards. The result is far from the Neo-Keynesians' ambition of 'fine tuning' economic activity. And the accumulating debt stores up further problems in the future.

The peculiarity of the political 'market'

The Public Choice School notes that decisions made through the political process are unlike decisions made in the marketplace, in two important respects.

First, in the marketplace, when someone pays for a something (a shoe repair, say), they receive the whole benefit (useable shoes). But in the political (or democratic) process, those who pay the costs are not always those who enjoy the benefits. If the government decides to build a new airport, for example, frequent air travellers will benefit; but the general public, including those who do not fly at all, will have to pay higher taxes; and those who live near the new airport will suffer the inconveniences of aircraft noise and local traffic congestion.

If people act in their own rational self-interest, as economists suggest, this division between benefits and costs must mean that electors would rationally vote for policies that benefit themselves while passing the cost on to others. Politicians, likewise, would rationally promote laws that benefit their own supporters but impose their costs on their opponents' supporters.

Second, in the commercial marketplace, the choices we make are not forced on anyone else. If you buy a pair of red shoes, for example, that does not stop anyone else buying shoes in black, brown or blue. But the choices made through the democratic process *are* imposed on others. If the majority decide to double military spending, pacifists accept that, and must contribute, unwillingly, to the costs.

In the political 'marketplace', therefore, each person's choices are critical to everyone else's welfare. The majority can impose their choices, and their costs, on the minority. At its most extreme, 50 + 1 per cent voters could impose their will on the other 50 − 1 per cent. No wonder that political debates often get so heated.

Self-interest in the political system

Politics might be less heated if everyone involved had the best interests of the community at heart. But Public Choice scholars argue that every part of the policymaking process is distorted by self-interest, prompting decisions that are not always optimal, rational or of general benefit.

Voter self-interest and ignorance

Elections, for example, are traditionally seen as tests of public opinion, and measures of the public interest. But individuals have many *different* opinions; and there is no single 'public interest', only many different, often *competing* interests. So we can expect electors to vote for parties and policies that they believe will benefit *themselves*, even if that would make others worse off. This is not a process that automatically maximises social welfare.

How elections are *structured* is also critical. A US-style first-past-the-post system, for instance, favours established parties, while EU-style transferable-voting systems favour minority parties. So, elections are not a definitive way of deciding economic or social policies; their outcome, and therefore the policies that are then adopted, depend very largely on what electoral structure is chosen.

There is another problem for those who place their faith in the democratic process to deliver sound economic and social policies. Such faith assumes that electors are *well informed* and *vote rationally*. The reality is that they are not and do not – for many reasons. First, your vote is unlikely to make a difference to whether your preferred candidate wins or not: the odds of it tipping the balance can be millions to one. Second, the majority may not elect your candidate anyway. Third, even if your candidate is elected, they may not actually deliver your preferred policy. Fourth, even if your candidate is elected and does deliver your policy, you cannot be sure exactly how much that policy will benefit you, nor how much it will ultimately cost you.

All these problems explain why real-world electors are so remarkably ignorant about what and who they are voting for. But this is *rational ignorance*, say Public Choice scholars. It is simply *not worth* electors spending time and effort researching the options on offer, because their vote is unlikely to make a difference, and the effects are unpredictable anyway.

Moreover, as the US economist Bryan Caplan (1971–) pointed out in *The Myth of the Rational Voter* (2017), electors' choices are strongly affected by a number of psychological biases. They dislike *job losses*, so vote to subsidise failing industries rather than for pro-productivity policies. They are *biased against foreigners*, seeing them as a threat to domestic jobs, so support protectionism rather than free trade. They worry about *immediate economic problems*, overlooking how things are generally improving. And they *underestimate the benefits of markets* and *overestimate the effectiveness of political solutions*.

Concentrated and diffused interests

Not only do the costs and benefits of public policy choices fall on different people; the benefits often go to a *small group* of people, while the costs are borne by a much larger number. This explains the prevalence of lobbying, and why interest groups can achieve an influence well beyond their numbers.

Lobbyists such as business associations and trade unions clearly have a strong interest in securing legislation that benefits their members – particularly if they can pass the costs on to the general public. And because the potential benefit is so *concentrated* among so few, it is easy for them to organise their members and raise funds for campaigning. This pursuit of privileges and benefits that are not worked for is called *rent seeking*.

For example, tomato growers have a *concentrated* interest in raising their profits. Being rational economic actors, they may campaign for tax breaks, production subsidies, minimum tomato prices or trade barriers against foreign tomatoes in the hope of convincing politicians to grant these favours. Being few in number, tomato growers are easy to organise, and the potential extra profit justifies them spending money on lobbying.

By contrast, the interests of the general public are diverse and *diffused*. Tomatoes are only one item in their shopping basket. If the growers succeed, shoppers may have to pay slightly more for tomatoes and get slightly less choice, but that is not worth them mobilising to oppose it.

The result is that vote-hungry politicians tend to favour the noisy special interest lobbies much more readily than they safeguard the 'silent majority' of the public. But as favours are granted to one group after another, the tax and regulatory systems grow more complex, competition is stifled, and the burdens on ordinary citizens keep rising.

The vote motive

Again using the tools of economics, Public Choice scholars suggest that the 'income' that rational self-interested politicians seek to maximise is *votes*. This *vote motive* means that political parties focus, not on their own loyalists who will probably vote for them anyway, but on winning support from the large body of *median voters* in the centre. And this explains the common complaint that there is little to choose between the parties.

Also, while customers in commercial markets can select any assortment of individual goods they wish, voters in the political market have to choose between only the few *policy packages* presented by the parties. And those again will be designed to win support from median voters. So electors who want different policy mixes – a party's defence plans, say, but not its welfare policy – remain unrepresented.

Then, once elected, politicians tend to vote for each other's legislative projects. 'You vote for my measure, and I will vote for yours' arrangements help them to get their own favoured proposals through the legislative process; but it leads to the creation of more laws and regulations than anyone really wants.

The bureaucracy

Public Choice scholars suggest that this excess of unrepresentative legislation is further distorted by the self-interest of public servants, who bring their own interests into the process.

For example, bureaucrats are likely to be much more expert than politicians on policy details. And when advising on laws and regulations, they have an interest in making each more intricate, because that justifies them demanding larger budgets and staff numbers. Complex rules also widen the scope for discretion – such as who might be entitled to benefits (e.g. grants) or subject to costs (e.g. fines). This discretionary function again justifies higher salaries; and in some countries, it allows bureaucrats to use their power corruptly, e.g. taking bribes in return for grants or fast-track processing of documents.

Again, because the bureaucrats involved in technical matters (e.g. food and drug safety or financial regulation) become so expert on those subjects, they often develop close relationships with people in the industries they are supposed to be regulating. They then become more willing to accept the industry's demands rather than standing up to them – a phenomenon known as *regulatory capture.*

Conclusion

Voters, politicians and officials may indeed act as rational self-interested economic agents. But, say Public Choice scholars, that produces an excess of over-complex legislation that often benefits special interests over those of the public. Markets may occasionally fail, but the failure of government is systemic. We should therefore be wary of calling upon it for action.

Decisions and constitutions

Decision-making costs and concerns

The democratic ideal is that, since collective decisions affect everyone, everyone should be involved in making those decisions. And ideally, everyone should agree, so that there is no risk of anyone being coerced or exploited by others.

But reaching 100 per cent agreement on anything is hard, since every decision could be blocked by any lone objector. So instead, we make collective choices by *majority vote* – usually by a *simple majority* – and accept the candidate with the largest number of votes, or the policy that gets 50 + 1 per cent (or more) in the legislature. But while this allows collective decisions to be made relatively easily, it leaves the possibility that a small majority (50 + 1 per cent) could exploit a significant minority (50 − 1 per cent) by voting themselves benefits at the expense of the others.

Only in rare cases (such as constitutional changes) do we demand a *qualified majority*, such as two-thirds of those voting. But some Public Choice scholars would like to see it used more widely. In deciding taxes, for example, it would be easy for a majority to place large burdens on the minority. The Nobel economist James Buchanan (1919–2013) suggested that to avoid this, tax changes should require something close to 100 per cent agreement, not the simple majority that decides them today.

Constitutional restraints

Buchanan's *tax constitution* is a particular case of the rules that (nearly) all countries have in place in order to give people (some) protection against majority exploitation. The US Constitution, for example, imposes a *division of powers* on decision makers, with *two legislative chambers* elected by different rules, a *President* who can *veto* controversial legislation, a *Supreme Court* to ensure that the rules are fairly interpreted and followed, and a *federal* structure in which some decisions are made locally rather than centrally.

Other countries have different restraints on majorities. Some, for example, have *proportional representation* electoral systems that empower minorities; and some have *qualified majority voting* on certain issues. The idea of these is that minorities should have some say in who is elected, even if that person is not their top choice, and some chance to block legislation that would damage them. Other jurisdictions have *direct democracy* systems such as voter initiatives, petitions, citizens' juries and referendums.

But there is no 'right' or 'wrong' voting system; as Public Choice scholars observe, each produces different results, and which is preferred is a matter of personal judgement rather than science. But economics can inform that choice by analysing what the outcomes might be.

The impact of the Public Choice School

Critics

While Public Choice theory has had a significant impact on academic and public policy debates, it has also faced criticism. Some economists argue that its 'rational self-interest' model of human behaviour is too simple and fails to encapsulate the many complex motivations that shape human decisions, and the multiplicity of ideological, moral, economic and social contexts that influence the policy debate. Such complexities, they say, also make it hard to test the theory empirically.

Others argue that while the theory might provide a useful caution about how policy is actually decided, that should not be exaggerated. Doing so could make people too sceptical about government action, leading to deficiencies such as the under-provision of public goods or inadequate checks on inequality.

Legacy

Despite such criticisms, Public Choice theory still accords with a general and increasing public scepticism about the political process, with its polarisation, horse trading, large bureaucracies, donor scandals, big business lobbying and corruption.

Public Choice has also been important in reminding economists of the potential pitfalls in translating academic ideas into practical policy. It has encouraged them to examine the incentives of everyone involved in the policymaking process, and to admit that the results may be different, even the opposite, of their intentions. It also reminds us that democracy works only if it is limited, both in terms of the range of its activities and its authority over minorities.

10 BEHAVIOURAL ECONOMICS

Behavioural Economics is an expanding field that uses psychology and cognitive science (the study of how people think) to explain how people make economic decisions. Rejecting the Classical and Neoclassical assumption that individuals rationally maximise their self-interest, it recognises that human decisions are often irrational, based on emotion, and influenced by external events and internal biases. All these, say behavioural economists, can produce suboptimal outcomes – both for the individual and for the wider public. But, some argue, by presenting choices in the right way, people can be 'nudged' into making better decisions.

Biases in human decision-making

The fact that human beings are not entirely *rational* agents who always strive to maximise their own satisfaction – but are instead emotional, prejudiced, easily distracted, impetuous and otherwise likely to make bad choices – has been obvious throughout history. But Behavioural Economics in its modern form arose in the mid twentieth century, when the American political scientist Herbert A. Simon (1916–2001) came up with an interesting explanation of how human beings *really* make decisions. They do not aim at making perfectly rational choices, he argued; rather, their aim is *satisficing* – to make a decision that is relatively easy but 'good enough' to serve their needs.

Satisficing is a matter of necessity: every day, we face a vast number of decisions, all presenting different options. It would be impossible to research every possibility in meticulous detail, then exhaustively map out the potential consequences of each, and finally make a rational choice between them. We have neither time nor brainpower for such a task.

Instead, said Simon, we rely on rules of thumb – *heuristics* – to help us make decisions quickly and without too much mental effort. We know this may not produce *perfect* decisions, nor fully rational and optimal ones. But if they are good enough, that is an acceptable trade-off. In the jargon, our decisions are a matter of *bounded rationality*: they are rational, but only within the *limits* of our knowledge, mental capacity and willingness to spend time and effort thinking about them.

The irrationality does not end there, though. Our rules of thumb might themselves be biased in one way or another, so producing systematically skewed decisions. For example, as Adam Smith recognised, people are usually overconfident about their abilities and their chances of success in a venture. And this *overconfidence bias* lures us into riskier behaviour than would be justified by an objective assessment of the situation.

Other biases in decision making

Our *cognitive biases* – biases in how we think and choose – were explored further by psychologists Daniel Kahneman (1934–2024) and Amos Tversky (1937–96). Among other things, they found that people tend to remember past mistakes and bad events more sharply than past successes and good events, and this *selective memory* skews their choices. Their recollection of headlines about plane crashes, for instance, makes them greatly overestimate the chance of one happening; and past headlines about company failures makes them overestimate the riskiness of investing in the stock market.

The effect is compounded by *loss aversion*, where we tend to be more strongly motivated to avoid losses than to acquire equivalent gains. This is why people buy insurance, even when the total they will pay in premiums over the years may come to more than the cost of what they are insuring. And it is why lotteries advertise huge jackpots: people know that the chance of winning is slight, so to persuade them to participate, the potential gain has to be far greater than their likely losses.

Particularly important to how individuals make economic and other decisions are *framing effects*. Their choices often reflect how the options are presented to them – the *choice architecture.* For example, because people are risk-averse, they are more likely to back a project or make an investment if they are told that it has a 75 per cent chance of success rather than a 25 per cent chance of failure. They are more likely to buy soap that is packaged as 'kind to your skin' than the same soap in a plain package. And they make more impulse buys, such as confectionary or gift cards, if shops place them near the checkout.

Another bias in human decision-making is *inertia*. We tend to stick with choices we have already made. Thus people who have placed their insurance with a particular company will tend to renew with the same company, even if the premiums rise (a fact that such companies exploit by offering cheap rates for new customers which they then raise significantly at renewal time).

Also, we tend to *accept decisions that others have made for us*. For example, if a firm auto-enrols its employees in a pension scheme (while giving them the option to decline), their participation is likely to be higher than if they have to enrol themselves in the same plan.

Linked to inertia is *familiarity bias*. Consumers often stick with familiar brands and are reluctant to try new ones, even if better choices are available, because this spares them the effort of researching the market. Likewise, investors tend to invest disproportionately in the home market, which they know, even though diversifying internationally may be a more rational strategy.

The *sunk cost* fallacy is similar. People tend to stick with a project – a business enterprise or an investment, say – because they have committed resources (e.g. time, money, emotion and effort) into it, rather than on its objective chances of delivering value.

Leading on from there is *confirmation bias*. People tend to give more credence and weight to information that justifies their existing choices, while discounting information to the contrary. For example, they are more likely to trust positive reviews for a product they prefer or an investment they have made, and to distrust negative ones.

People's choices are also influenced by how and when information is delivered. The *salience* effect means that we give more weight to information that is prominent or emotionally gripping, even if it is not genuinely important or relevant to a decision. For example, people may be drawn to products or causes because of a recent, striking advertising campaign.

Allied to this is the *availability bias*, that people rely more on information that comes easily to mind, such as an advertisement, even an old one, with a catchy jingle.

Peer pressure too influences people's decisions. Thus, consumers are more likely to purchase brands, such as clothing styles and fashion labels, that are favoured by others in their social group. *Social norms* also exert significant pressure. For example, people may avoid careers that are legal and rewarding but are not considered respectable by their community, such as working in the adult entertainment, lobbying or debt collection industries.

Social pressures can also produce a *herd mentality*. Investors may buy or sell particular stocks because others are doing the same, even though the underlying financials do not support such a decision. This can lead to asset bubbles (like the 'tulip mania' of the 1630s or the 'dotcom boom' of the late 1990s) in which prices reach unjustified and unsustainable levels. It can also lead to bank crashes (e.g. the 1980s' US Savings & Loan Crisis) as people rush to withdraw their funds from what is perceived as a troubled institution – thereby worsening the problem.

Another source of poor economic decision-making is the *endowment effect*. People tend to place a higher value on things they own or inherit, rather than assigning them a more objective value. That can make people reluctant to part with assets that they rationally should sell.

There is also a *time bias*. People prefer smaller but immediate rewards over larger but delayed rewards. Thus, companies that are hoping to attract customers into long-term contracts might offer an immediate 'cashback' or 'joining gift' to sweeten the decision.

Anchoring bias is where individuals tend to rely more heavily on information that they encounter early on in the decision-making process. This information (the *anchor*) may be irrelevant or arbitrary, yet it colours subsequent evaluations. For example, a retailer may quote a high 'recommended price' on which they then offer discounts: the high initial price suggests to consumers that the product is actually worth more than they have to pay.

Mental accounting is another bias, where people mentally partition their money into notional 'accounts' with different sources, uses or attributes. For example, when people receive unexpected windfalls, such as a tax refund, they may be more willing to 'splurge' that money on extravagant holidays, luxuries or entertainments rather than save it or buy better-quality everyday goods.

Implications of thought biases

Contrary to the traditional economic assumption of rational self-interest, therefore, Behavioural Economics suggests that people's choices are often heavily skewed by biases in their thinking, by pressures from those around them and by how choices are presented. But if people make poor economic decisions because of this, then their welfare, and that of the community around them, will suffer. The question for economists is then how to compensate for people's cognitive biases and improve the choice architecture such that their decisions become more optimal and welfare-generating. This issue has consequences in many economic situations, including finance, product marketing, business management and public policy.

Behavioural finance

In finance, the growing field of *behavioural finance* brings psychological factors into the study of financial markets (including personal saving, investor behaviour and debt management). It has helped financial practitioners to develop investment strategies – known as 'de-biasing' – that mitigate people's prejudices (particularly to counteract the excessive influence of loss aversion).

Behavioural Economics has also enabled financial regulators to improve investor protection, product suitability and market stability. By appreciating how investors' biases may lead to suboptimal financial decisions, regulators can help protect them, e.g. by restricting high risk products or demanding that customers are given fuller information. By understanding herd behaviour, regulators may also be able to improve market stability through 'circuit breaker' strategies. And they can help to ensure products genuinely meet investors' needs by curbing practices that exploit their behavioural biases.

Product marketing

Behavioural Economics can help marketers create more effective messaging. For example, they might highlight the potential *losses* of *not* purchasing a product; or capitalise on brand loyalty; or make packaging more salient and attractive; or engage peer pressure with customer testimonials, celebrity endorsements and social media reviews.

Marketers can also improve sales by understanding how customers really respond to prices (as opposed to how most economic textbooks assume they do). As mentioned, for instance, they might state an initially high 'anchor' price to serve as a reference point that influences how customers regard the quality of the product.

Behavioural Economics can also help marketers to design better online sales sites – say, with 'favourites' to exploit inertia. It can help retailers to increase revenues by suggesting the best position for goods, such as placing higher-margin products at eye level, or complementary goods (e.g. cheese and crackers) near each other.

Business management

In business, understanding human biases and rule-of-thumb heuristics can help team leaders improve collaboration and compensate for the cognitive biases of individual team members. It can also help in structuring incentives, such as in pay packages. And it can help managers select better job candidates by overcoming their biases in framing job advertisements and assessing applicants.

In addition, understanding the influence of social norms, framing effects and other biases may help businesses improve their communication strategies with both public and employees.

Public policy and nudge

Behavioural Economics can also inform public policy and help design better programmes to improve citizens' health, welfare and retirement security, and improve financial regulation, consumer protection and economic stability. It can help governments communicate more effectively and frame their policy initiatives to make them more acceptable to the public.

By adjusting the choice architecture, governments can 'nudge' people into socially desirable behaviours – an approach developed by US legal scholar Cass Sunstein (1954–) and economist Richard Thaler (1945–) in their 2008 book, *Nudge*. For example, by making organ donation the default option on driving licence applications (harnessing *inertia*), the participation in such programmes is significantly increased. Health warnings on salty or fatty foods, or on tobacco products (employing *loss aversion*), can prompt people to reduce their consumption of these items. And placing healthier foodstuffs at the front of the counter when school children select their lunchtime meal can prompt them to choose those options.

Richard Thaler used nudge theory to propose another important policy, aimed at increasing employee retirement saving, the Save More Tomorrow ('SMarT') Plan. Employees are asked to increase their savings contributions at some future date, such as when they get a pay rise. This takes advantage of the fact that people are more willing to make sacrifices in the future than now; and it avoids *loss aversion* because workers know that, after a pay rise, they will still be better off. Studies suggest that SMarT plans raise savings rates significantly, with participation rates almost double traditional plans, adding tens of billions more dollars to US workers' retirement assets.

Sunstein and Thaler are clear, however, that to be a *nudge*, rather than a *compulsion*, the intervention must be cheaply and easily avoidable. Thus, making healthier food easier to reach is a nudge; banning salty fried snacks is not. Putting health warnings on tobacco products is a nudge; making people fill in a long health questionnaire before they can buy tobacco is not.

General criticism and legacy

Nevertheless, some critics claim that government 'nudges' too often stray over the line and become compulsions. They say that altering the choice architecture may *limit* choice and that attempts to manipulate citizens' choices are paternalist and illegitimate. The manipulation may not even be obvious to those affected, making it hard for them to object. And the same nudge may have different (even potentially undesirable) consequences in different places, cultures or circumstances, making it a dangerous policy.

More generally, mainstream economists say that Behavioural Economics lacks a unified theory. It is too dependent on context and culture, with its conclusions too often being overgeneralised from one-off experiments with (unrepresentative) Western student volunteers who are asked to make unrealistically simple choices. To the critics, therefore, this is not an approach that can be applied in complex situations across all cultures or used confidently to predict and influence the future.

The spread of behavioural thinking in economics has not completely supplanted the traditional 'rational maximising actor' model, which mainstream economists still see as a useful abstraction that helps guide macroeconomic policy. And even if *individuals* do not behave entirely rationally, the competitive pressures of the market may still drive *overall* behaviour towards the optimal, utility-maximising outcomes predicted by the standard theory.

Nevertheless, a growing corpus of empirical studies make it difficult to dismiss the significance of psychological factors in shaping people's economic behaviour. The question is how far these factors can be generalised across populations and cultures, and how legitimate are the policy interventions based on them.

11 THE FUTURE AND THE PAST

Future schools of thought?

People have been trying to understand – and control – economic life for at least forty centuries. In that time, a wide range of theories and perspectives has developed. So, what future schools of thought might emerge?

The future is impossible to predict. But economic thinking will be shaped by future challenges, just as it has been in the past – with the Classical economists trying to understand production and value, the Neoclassicals trying to understand how markets work, the Keynesians trying to smooth out economic cycles, the Public Choice school looking at how economic policy really operates, and so on.

With our better understanding of human diversity, partly the result of our more mobile and connected world, economists may delve further into psychological explanations of real-world phenomena such as why people panic-buy in crises or stick to bad investments, and how context (such as culture and institutions) affect human choices.

Improvements in data collection and analysis will probably shape future economic thought, just as it bolstered the Keynesian analysis. But such is the fine 'granularity' of the data produced today that the focus might be more on making micro-predictions in very local circumstances, rather than attempting to predict whole economies.

Allied to this, there may be more focus on decentralised decision-making. The sharing economy of Uber, Lyft, AirBnB, TaskRabbit and others may draw economists' focus from centralised systems and policymaking and towards polycentric systems and local decision-making, and onto related issues like how such systems generate trust among customers.

Other technological developments may lead economists in yet other directions. There may be more attention on the effects of AI on employment, including professional tasks such as preparing legal documents, medical diagnostics, teaching, and much else. The rise of cryptocurrencies may raise new issues and pose a challenge to economists' traditional thinking on monetary management.

Issues around a growing and more mobile human population may lead to an increasing focus on the use and pricing of resources such as land and water. And with some of the poorest countries now becoming much richer due to globalised trade, greater attention may be focused on the role of these economies within the world trading and production network.

Conclusion: strength through diversity

The history of economic thought is marked by a rich diversity of perspectives, each with its own strengths and limitations, and each making important contributions to our understanding of how economies function and how individuals make economic decisions.

It is impossible to predict what events will unfold and what future schools of economic thought may emerge. But the study of economics, and our understanding of economic life, will undoubtedly expand with each new perspective. In the past, each school of thought has brought its own unique ideas to the debates on value, exchange, prices, decision-making and the role of government, helping us to understand how economic life works. New schools of thought will further expand that understanding.

Diverse viewpoints mean there will never be a single, unified theory of economics that can account for all the complexities of the real world. But the coexistence of various schools of thought has been highly productive in improving this understanding. By engaging with and critiquing one another, economists have been able to refine their analytical tools, challenge assumptions, reduce error and develop more sophisticated approaches to economic issues.

The strength of economics as a field of investigation lies in its pluralism and willingness to engage with different perspectives. In disagreeing about things, economists can hone their ideas and so improve their understanding of economic phenomena. And hopefully, their appreciation of the past mistakes of so many great economic thinkers will remind them of the limitations of any attempt to explain something so complex and dynamic as human economic activity.

REFERENCES

Bastiat, F. (1846, 1848) *Economic Sophisms*. (Originally published as articles in the *Journal des Économistes* and collected as *Sophismes Économiques*. Paris: Guillaumin & Co., Libraires-Éditeurs.

Bastiat, F. (1850) *That Which Is Seen, and That Which Is Not Seen*. (Originally published as *Ce Qu'on Voit et Ce Qu'on Ne Voit Pas, ou L'Economie Politique en une Leçon*). Paris: Librarie de Guillaumin & Co.

Bastiat, F. (1850) *The Law*. (Originally published as *La Loi*.) Paris: Librarie de Guillaumin & Co.

Buchanan, J. M. and Wagner, R. (1977) *Democracy in Deficit: The Political Legacy of Lord Keynes*. New York: Academic Press.

Caplan, B. (2017) *The Myth of the Rational Voter*. Princeton University Press.

Fisher, I. (1930) *The Theory of Interest*. New York: Macmillan.

Friedman, M. (1957) *A Theory of the Consumption Function*. Princeton University Press.

Friedman, M. and Schwartz, A. J. (1992) *A Monetary History of the United States, 1867–1960*. National Bureau of Economic Research.

Jevons, W. S. (1871) *The Theory of Political Economy*. London: Macmillan.

Keynes, J. M. (1923) *A Tract on Monetary Reform*. London: Macmillan.

Keynes, J. M. (1936) *The General Theory of Employment, Interest, and Money.* Palgrave Macmillan.

Magness, P. W. and Mokovi, M. (2021) The mainstreaming of Marx: the effect of the Russian Revolution on Karl Marx's influence. *Journal of Political Economy* 131(6): 2023.

Malthus, T. R. (1798) *An Essay on the Principle of Population.* London: J. Johnson.

Marshall, A. (1890) *Principles of Economics.* London: Macmillan.

Marx, K. H. (1867) *Das Kapital.* Verlag von Otto Meisner.

Menger, C. (1871) *Principles of Economics.* (Originally published as Grundsätze der Volkswirtschaftslehre.) Vienna: Wilhelm Braumüller.

Mill, J. (1821) *Elements of Political Economy.* London: Baldwin, Craddock, and Joy.

Mises, L. von (1949) *Human Action.* Yale University Press.

Ricardo, D. (1817) *On the Principles of Political Economy and Taxation.* London: John Murray.

Smith, A. (1776) *An Inquiry into the Nature and Causes of the Wealth of Nations.* London: W. Strachan and T. Cadell.

Sunstein, C. R. and Thaler, R. H. (2018) *Nudge: Improving Decisions about Health, Wealth and Happiness.* London: Penguin.

Further reading

General

Landes, D. S. (1998) *The Wealth and Poverty of Nations.* Abacus.

North, D. C. (1981) *Structure and Change in Economic History.* W. W. Norton.

Skousen, M. (2022) *The Making of Modern Economics.* London: Routledge.

Sowell, T. (2014) *Basic Economics*. Basic Books.

Preclassical economics

Grice-Hutchinson, M. (2012) *Early Economic Thought in Spain 1177–1740*. Routledge.

Hirschfield, M. L. (2018) *Aquinas and the Market: Toward a Humane Economy*. Harvard University Press.

LeHaye, L. (2008) Mercantilism. In *The Encyclopaedia of Economics* (ed. D. R. Henderson). Indianapolis, IN: Liberty Fund.

Selkirk, A. (2020) *The Secret of Civilization* (http://www.civilization.org.uk).

The Classical School

Butler, E. (2007) *Adam Smith – A Primer*. London: Institute of Economic Affairs.

Butler, E. (2011) *The Condensed Wealth of Nations*. London: Adam Smith Institute.

Robbins, L. (1952) *The Theory of Economic Policy*. London: Macmillan.

Sowell, T. (2006) *On Classical Economics*. Yale University Press.

Karl Marx

Foley, D. K. (2009) *Understanding* Capital*: Marx's Economic Theory*. Harvard University Press.

The Neoclassical synthesis

Samuelson, P. A. (1948) *Economics*. New York: McGraw-Hill.

Keynes and the Keynesians

Hansen, A. (1953) *A Guide to Keynes*. New York: McGraw-Hill.

Hayek, F. A. (2009) *A Tiger by the Tail: The Keynesian Legacy of Inflation*. London: Institute of Economic Affairs.

The Chicago School

Butler, E. (2011) *Milton Friedman: A Concise Guide to the Ideas and Influence of the Free-Market Economist*. Petersfield, UK: Harriman House.

Friedman, M. with Friedman, R. (1962) *Capitalism and Freedom*. University of Chicago Press.

Friedman, M. and Friedman, R. (1990) *Free to Choose*. Mariner Books (reprint).

Van Overtveld, J. (2009) *The Chicago School: How the University of Chicago Assembled the Thinkers who Revolutionized Economics and Business*. Chicago, IL: Agate B2.

The Public Choice School

Boudreaux, D. J. and Holcombe, R. G. (2021) *The Essential James Buchanan*. Vancouver, BC: Fraser Institute.

Butler, E. (2012) *Public Choice – A Primer*. London: Institute of Economic Affairs.

Caplan, B. (2017) *The Myth of the Rational Voter*. Princeton University Press.

Olson, M. (1974) *The Logic of Collective Action: Public Goods and the Theory of Groups*. Harvard University Press.

The Austrian School

Butler, E. (2010) *Austrian Economics – A Primer*. Adam Smith Institute.

Butler, E. (2010) *Ludwig von Mises – A Primer*. London: Institute of Economic Affairs.

Butler, E. (2012) *Friedrich Hayek*. London: Pan Macmillan.

Coyne, C. J. and Boettke, P. J. (2020) *The Essential Austrian Economics*. Vancouver, BC: Fraser Institute.

Ebeling, R. (2016) *Austrian Economics and Public Policy*. Fairfax, VA: Future of Freedom Foundation.

Horwitz, S. (2020) *A Guide to Austrian Economics*. Washington DC: Cato Institute.

Mises, L. von (2010) *Economic Policy*. Indianapolis, IN: Liberty Fund.

Behavioural Economics

Akerlof, G. A. and Shiller, R. J. (2015) *Phishing for Phools: The Economics of Manipulation and Deception*. Princeton University Press.

Sunstein, C. R. and Thaler, R. H. (2018) *Nudge: Improving Decisions about Health, Wealth and Happiness*. London: Penguin.

ABOUT THE IEA

The Institute of Economic Affairs is a research and educational charity (No. CC 235 351). Its mission is to improve understanding of the fundamental institutions of a free society by analysing and expounding the role of markets in solving economic and social problems.

The IEA achieves its mission through:

- a high-quality publishing programme
- conferences, seminars, lectures and other events
- outreach to school and university students
- appearances across print, broadcast and digital media

The IEA, established in 1955 by the late Sir Antony Fisher, is an educational charity, not a political organisation. It is independent of any political party or group and does not carry on activities intended to affect support for any political party or candidate in any election or referendum, or at any other time. It is financed by sales of publications, conference fees and voluntary donations.

In addition to its main series of publications, the IEA publishes the academic journal *Economic Affairs* in partnership with the University of Buckingham.

The IEA is aided in its work by an Academic Advisory Council and a panel of Honorary Fellows. Together with other academics, they review prospective IEA publications, their comments being passed on anonymously to authors. All IEA papers are therefore subject to the same rigorous, independent refereeing process as used by leading academic journals.

IEA publications are often used in classrooms and incorporated into school and university courses. They are also sold throughout the world and often translated and reprinted. The IEA supports and works with a global network of like-minded organisations, through its Initiative for African Trade and Prosperity, EPICENTER and other international programmes.

Views expressed in the IEA's publications are those of the authors, not those of the Institute (which has no corporate view), its Managing Trustees, Academic Advisory Council members or senior staff. Members of the Institute's Academic Advisory Council, Honorary Fellows, Trustees and Staff are listed on the following page.

The Institute gratefully acknowledges financial support for its publications programme and other work from a generous benefaction by the late Professor Ronald Coase.

The Institute of Economic Affairs
2 Lord North Street, Westminster, London SW1P 3LB
Tel: 020 7799 8900
Email: iea@iea.org.uk
Web: iea.org.uk

Executive Director and Ralph Harris Fellow Tom Clougherty

Editorial Director Dr Kristian Niemietz

Managing Trustees
Chairman: Linda Edwards
Kevin Bell
Professor Christian Bjørnskov
Robert Boyd
Robin Edwards
Tom Harris
Professor Patrick Minford
Bruno Prior
Professor Martin Ricketts

Life Vice Presidents and former Chairmen of the IEA Board of Trustees
Lord Vinson
Professor D R Myddelton
Neil Record

Academic Advisory Council
Chairman: Professor Christian Bjørnskov
Dr Mikko Arevuo
Graham Bannock
Dr Roger Bate
Professor Alberto Benegas-Lynch, Jr
Professor Donald J Boudreaux
Professor John Burton
Professor Forrest Capie
Dr Juan Castaneda
Professor Steven N S Cheung
Dr Billy Christmas
Professor David Collins
Professor Tim Congdon
Professor Christopher Coyne
Professor David de Meza
Professor Kevin Dowd
Professor David Greenaway
Dr Ingrid A Gregg
Dr Samuel Gregg
Professor Steve H Hanke
Professor Keith Hartley
Dr Jerry Jordan
Professor Syed Kamall
Professor Terence Kealey
Dr Lynne Kiesling
Professor Daniel B Klein
Dr Benedikt Koehler
Dr Mark Koyama
Professor Chandran Kukathas
Dr Andrew Lilico
Professor Stephen C Littlechild
Dr Eileen Marshall
Dr Matthew McCaffrey
Dr John Meadowcroft
Dr Anja Merz
Dr Lucy Minford
Professor Patrick Minford
Professor Julian Morris
Professor Alan Morrison
Professor D R Myddelton
Dr Marie Newhouse
Dr Chris O'Leary
Paul Ormerod
Dr Neema Parvini
Professor Mark Pennington
Professor Srinivasa Rangan
Professor Martin Ricketts
Dr Alex Robson
Professor Pascal Salin
Dr Razeen Sally
Professor Pedro Schwartz Giron
Professor J R Shackleton
Professor Jane S Shaw Stroup
Professor W Stanley Siebert
Professor Andrew Smith
Dr Carlo Stagnaro
Professor Elaine Sternberg
Professor James Tooley
Professor Nicola Tynan
Professor Roland Vaubel
Dr Cento Veljanovski
Professor Lawrence H White
Professor Geoffrey E Wood

Honorary Fellows
Professor Michael Beenstock
Professor Richard A Epstein
Professor David Laidler
Professor Deirdre McCloskey
Professor Vernon L Smith

Other books recently published by the IEA include:

School of Thought: 101 Great Liberal Thinkers
Eamonn Butler
ISBN 978-0-255-36776-9; £12.50

Raising the Roof: How to Solve the United Kingdom's Housing Crisis
Edited by Jacob Rees-Mogg and Radomir Tylecote
ISBN 978-0-255-36782-0; £12.50

How Many Light Bulbs Does It Take to Change the World?
Matt Ridley and Stephen Davies
ISBN 978-0-255-36785-1; £10.00

The Henry Fords of Healthcare ... Lessons the West Can Learn from the East
Nima Sanandaji
ISBN 978-0-255-36788-2; £10.00

An Introduction to Entrepreneurship
Eamonn Butler
ISBN 978-0-255-36794-3; £12.50

An Introduction to Democracy
Eamonn Butler
ISBN 978-0-255-36797-4; £12.50

Having Your Say: Threats to Free Speech in the 21st Century
Edited by J. R. Shackleton
ISBN 978-0-255-36800-1; £17.50

The Sharing Economy: Its Pitfalls and Promises
Michael C. Munger
ISBN 978-0-255-36791-2; £12.50

An Introduction to Trade and Globalisation
Eamonn Butler
ISBN 978-0-255-36803-2; £12.50

Why Free Speech Matters
Jamie Whyte
ISBN 978-0-255-36806-3; £10.00

The People Paradox: Does the World Have Too Many or Too Few People?
Steven E. Landsburg and Stephen Davies
ISBN 978-0-255-36809-4; £10.00

An Introduction to Economic Inequality
Eamonn Butler
ISBN 978-0-255-36815-5; £10.00

Carbon Conundrum: How to Save Climate Change Policy from Government Failure
Philip Booth and Carlo Stagnaro
ISBN 978-0-255-36812-4; £12.50

Scaling the Heights: Thought Leadership, Liberal Values and the History of The Mont Pelerin Society
Eamonn Butler
ISBN 978-0-255-36818-6; £10.00

Faith in Markets? Abrahamic Religions and Economics
Edited by Benedikt Koehler
ISBN 978-0-255-36824-7; £17.50

Human Nature and World Affairs: An Introduction to Classical Liberalism and International Relations Theory
Edwin van de Haar
ISBN 978-0-255-36827-8; £15.00

The Experience of Free Banking
Edited by Kevin Dowd
ISBN 978-0-255-36830-8; £25.00

Apocalypse Next: The Economics of Global Catastrophic Risks
Stephen Davies
ISBN 978-0-255-36821-6; £17.50

New Paternalism Meets Older Wisdom: Looking to Smith and Hume on Rationality, Welfare and Behavioural Economics
Erik W. Matson
ISBN 978-0-255-36833-9; £12.50

An Introduction to Taxation
Eamonn Butler
ISBN 978-0-255-36836-0; £12.50

Imperial Measurement: A Cost–Benefit Analysis of Western Colonialism
Kristian Niemietz
ISBN 978-0-255-36839-1; £10.00

The Quantity Theory of Money: A New Restatement
Tim Congdon
ISBN 978-0-255-36842-1; £15.00

Unions Resurgent? The Past, Present and Uncertain Future of Trade Unions in Britain
J. R. Shackleton
ISBN 978-0-255-36845-2; £15.00

Other IEA publications

Comprehensive information on other publications and the wider work of the IEA can be found at www.iea.org.uk. To order any publication please see below.

Personal customers

Orders from personal customers should be directed to the IEA:

IEA
2 Lord North Street
Westminster
London SW1P 3LB
Tel: 020 7799 8911
Email: accounts@iea.org.uk

Trade customers

All orders from the book trade should be directed to the IEA's distributor:

Ingram Publisher Services UK
1 Deltic Avenue
Rooksley
Milton Keynes MK13 8LD
Tel: 01752 202301
Email: ipsuk.orders@ingramcontent.com

IEA subscriptions

The IEA offers a subscription service. For £350 a year, UK-based subscribers will receive every book the IEA publishes along with invitations to IEA events – while also supporting the IEA's charitable mission. You can subscribe online by becoming a 'Founding Insider' at insider.iea.org.uk. Otherwise, please contact:

Subscriptions
IEA
2 Lord North Street
Westminster
London SW1P 3LB
Tel: 020 7799 8911
Email: accounts@iea.org.uk